THE PRACTICE
OF ATTENTION

Also by Cody Cook-Parrott

A Sacred Shift: A Book About Personal Practice

*How to Not Always Be Working: A Toolkit
for Creativity and Radical Self-Care*

*Getting to Center: Pathways to Finding
Yourself Within the Great Unknown*

Look About You: A Book of Ordinary Prayers

Praise for *The Practice of Attention*

"When our attention splinters, so do we. Cody's work—this book—is the thread that sewed me back together. It is not an exaggeration to say this book will save your life. It saved mine."

HOLLY WHITAKER
New York Times bestselling author of *Quit Like A Woman*

"The only book we need right now."

SAMANTHA IRBY
New York Times bestselling author of *We Are Never Meeting in Real Life* and *Quietly Hostile*

"Cody Cook-Parrott has written a beautiful book about the importance of attention and how we might turn to it in a world that is endlessly trying to capture ours. Cody doesn't try to convince you to turn your attention toward only things that can be monetized or things that are capital-P Productive. I love the way this gorgeous book reminds us that the beauty of nature is as worthy of our attention as so many other ways in which we spend our days. I will gift this book to many, and I am grateful for its existence."

ESMÉ WEIJUN WANG
New York Times bestselling author of *The Collected Schizophrenias*

"Cody has created a road map for reclaiming the most precious of resources: our time on this planet and our impact upon it."

"With *The Practice of Attention*, Cody Cook-Parrott offers pathways of reflection and reclamation in a world that constantly pulls us away from the sacred. This is a book of practical reminders and artistic rituals for body, mind, and spirit. Cody delivers the simple and the profound in one place, giving us the gift of their accessible language and vulnerable process. Staying present isn't easy work, but it is possible with intentional effort and creative determination. With their generous and radical honesty, Cody Cook-Parrott exemplifies the hope and freedom resulting from the necessary undertaking of reclaiming attention."

"The tools in this book have radically reshaped my creative practice. I love how Cody unpacks the inner and outer forces that distract us from what really matters. Their invitations to audit our attention, reconnect with our bodies, and cultivate a creative research process are essential for every artist."

"*The Practice of Attention* has a big heart. It is not a book to read quickly and check off the to-do list. Instead, it is a book to be savored. We are encouraged to slow down, find presence, and listen deeply. Cody offers compassionate guidance and generous practices that we can weave into our daily lives to reinvigorate the strength and capacity of attention. In these pages we find a compass that will bring us back to our power, again and again."

LIZ MIGLIORELLI

herbalist, educator, storyteller

"Cody guides us gently and generously toward an approach to attention rooted in integrity. Their attention practices attend to the maker, student, teacher, and neighbor in us all, reminding us that attention is, at root, a connective force."

TAMARA SANITBAÑEZ

writer and artist

"If you've ever deleted an app and still felt restless, *The Practice of Attention* will make sense of that feeling. Cody Cook-Parrott helps us move into what's next, like a soft, gentle path through the woods, exploring areas like movement, community, creativity, and faith grounded in both practice and in spirit."

SETH WERKHEISER

Social Media Escape Club

"*The Practice of Attention* is a warm and gentle appeal for how (and why) to live a more embodied, human life. In a world that is often noisy, distracted, and filled with screens and apps that scream for (and monetize) our attention, Cody has given us a book brimming with thoughtful questions, practical tips, and poetic inspiration that all come together to form a welcome pathway back to the self. Experiment with even one of the suggestions in these pages and you will find yourself changed."

NIC ANTOINETTE

writer

"In a world engineered to buy and sell our time, *The Practice of Attention* is a tender, luminous guide to the art of focus as an act of resistance. Through vivid storytelling and creative exercises, Cody Cook-Parrott offers an honest and compassionate roadmap out of distraction and back into connection—with ourselves, our work, and one another."

ELLEN RUTT

artist

"Reading *The Practice of Attention* feels like the best kind of conversation—inspiring, human, deep, full of curiosity. Cody writes to us all as if we are their dearest friend. It's clear they want us to thrive, and this book is an invitation to meet them in the aliveness they have cultivated over many years of exploration. *The Practice of Attention* is grounded in love, spirit, and sweetness while not turning away from the complexities of being human. Full of tangible actions, prompts, and questions—my book is tattered, dog-eared, and underlined."

CHELSEA GRANGER

artist

"Less screen time rocks, but why exactly? And what for? What means the most to you in your life? Reading *The Practice of Attention* gave me the desire and the courage to excavate my relationship with my distractions, good and bad. Through Cody's story, I realized that my innate calling to reclaim my attention is not simply about time and creating more of it so that I may be more ambitious, productive, or prolific. This book helped me understand that my constant sense of yearning is actually connected to my desire for concentration and the healing power of focus. Cody's fearless inventory was both an invitation and a push for me to open, to channel, and to remember my life happens once."

SKY FUSCO

artist

THE PRACTICE OF ATTENTION

CULTIVATING PRESENCE IN A DISTRACTED WORLD

CODY COOK-PARROTT

ST. MARTIN'S
ESSENTIALS
NEW YORK

Published in the United States by St. Martin's Essentials, an imprint of St. Martin's Publishing Group

EU Representative: Macmillan Publishers Ireland Ltd, 1st Floor, The Liffey Trust Centre, 117–126 Sheriff Street Upper, Dublin 1, D01 YC43

This book is not intended as a substitute for the medical recommendations of physicians, mental health professionals, or other health-care providers. Rather, it is intended to offer information to help the reader cooperate with physicians, mental health professionals, and health-care providers in a mutual quest for optimal well-being. We advise readers to carefully review and understand the ideas presented and to seek the advice of a qualified professional before attempting to use them.

Cover and jacket design by Charli Barnes
Book design by Rachael Murray

www.stmartins.com

The Library of Congress Cataloging-in-Publication Data is available upon request.

ISBN 978-1-64963-414-6 (trade paperback)

ISBN 978-1-64963-415-3 (ebook)

Our books may be purchased in bulk for specialty retail/wholesale, literacy, corporate/premium, educational, and subscription box use. Please contact MacmillanSpecialMarkets@macmillan.com.

First Edition: 2026

10 9 8 7 6 5 4 3 2 1

Attention, taken to its highest degree, is the same thing as prayer. It presupposes faith and love.
Absolutely unmixed attention is prayer.
If we turn our mind toward the good, it is impossible that little by little the whole soul will not be attracted thereto in spite of itself.

—Simone Weil, *Gravity and Grace*

CONTENTS

INTRODUCTION

One might assume that a book about attention should be written by someone who studies attention, but I'd argue that it should be written by someone who studies art. With that in mind, this book details how I, an interdisciplinary artist, reclaimed my own attention and how art-making, ritual, and research brought me back to what I was hungry for: honesty and unbroken focus in my work. To make anything with heart and quality, our brains must keep a steady focus for more than a few minutes, and my attention was fractured seemingly beyond repair. Emphasizing daily creative acts is what healed me and returned me to a state of delight.

This book is not meant to be a "how-to" guide. Rather, it is a recounting of how I got here, to a place of focused attention on what matters most to me, and it is a pathway for how you can get to this place as well. It is a retelling of how I crawled my way out of social media and technology addiction after using them to build my career and how I slowly built back the muscles I use to stay devoted to my work, relationships, and creative life.

Just like a fitness regimen, this required strenuous activity and disciplined action. There was no magic drug, perfect routine, or fast-acting supplement that cured me. Time, dedication, and self-forgiveness were at the heart of my revival. I had to build practices that turned me toward spirit and myself. I had to lean on my community to restore my sense of self-worth and belonging, and I had to embrace my need for companionship, connection, and care. All of this showed me a landscape of abundance that was beyond what I could have imagined when I was buried in my phone.

REBUILDING ATTENTION

The process of rebuilding my attention was interconnected with my work to release people-pleasing and perfectionism, both professionally and personally. In order to find presence, I had to completely detach from what other people thought of me and how they thought I should live my life. Instead, I had to fully trust my inner knowing, skills, and creative abilities, which allowed my creative energy to flow freely in all areas of life, from my work and friendships to my spirituality and service to others.

In her book *The Serviceberry*, Robin Wall Kimmerer writes, "The excess in my life tends to be books, because people are always giving them to me. So when I turn to the last page—or sometimes well before—I might give a book to a friend. You do it too. That simple act is the atom of a gift economy." She goes on to describe that this is not so different than what the serviceberries are doing, and how we can always be learning from the land. While I am often referencing the attention economy in this book, I am also deeply thinking about the gift economy—how we gift our resources, time, and energy.

Anti-perfectionism is at the core of everything I teach and write about. It is the center of the wheel we turn to get ourselves out of self-deprecation and self-pity so we can find our way toward more focused creativity and attention. It is how we take stock of our privilege and unwind our biases so we can become more fully a part of society. It is how we become thoughtful caretakers of the world. When we are willing to make mistakes and take risks, we are in the chorus of the song of attention.

This work began for me fourteen years ago when I first entered recovery from alcoholism, found solace and god in anonymous twelve-step fellowships, defined my own Higher Power, and cleaned up my relationship to substances, money, and other people. This work gave me my life back, and in many ways, this book is a reflection of that reclamation. My addiction to alcohol was absolutely killing me, and I needed complete abstinence to survive its cunning, baffling, and powerful ways. And, to be honest, our collective addiction to apps and our phones are not that far away from the phenomenon of craving we see with drugs and alcohol.

In the past, I was often able to take breaks from social media and abstain from its use in a similar way to how

I approached my alcohol recovery, but I found that my mindset around it still needed tending to. I used to become obsessed with the idea of posting, receiving likes, and getting dopamine hits. This was a parallel experience to when I first tried to quit drinking. I could go a few days or even a few months, but I was always thinking about the next drink in the same way I was always thinking about the next post. If this sounds like your relationship with social media, I want to assure you that you do not have to live this way.

Whether it's alcohol, drugs, food, sex, or social media that is stealing your attention, addiction sweeps us out of our lives and into unnecessary chaos. And while chaos is often a natural part of life to foster growth and progress, this self-inflicted chaos tends to lead us down dark paths of shame, self-neglect, and guilt. Luckily, there are swift and graceful ways out of these cycles, and it involves moving our attention from what doesn't serve us toward spirit, toward the self, and toward our communities. Tending to our addictive tendencies, whether they majorly impact our lives or not, is vital in bringing us out of ourselves and into the world so we may honor and embrace our true selves. I have found that prayer, contact with my Higher Power, and the fellowship of other people have worked wonders in making my life infinitely more spacious in this way.

If talk of spirituality in general has put a bad taste in your mouth, I hear you. Don't turn away just yet. Follow me down this path of questioning and curiosity so you can uncover more about yourself through a personalized, spiritual lens. There are so many ways to define god, service, and togetherness. And there are infinite ways to tap into source and bring your attention back to your creativity and essential work. By the end of this book, it is my greatest wish that you will find less pull toward your screens and vices and more pull toward what means the most to you in life.

WHY THIS BOOK? WHY NOW?

While my own story of art practice began as a dancer, writing has been the ultimate and consistent through-line of my career and studies. In order to do this, I have used digital platforms and technology considerably to connect with others and share my work with the world. With this being said, I want to be clear that this is not a book about shutting everything down, moving into a cabin in the woods, and never talking to people again, and this book is certainly not anti-technology. Rather, this is a call for us to reimagine how we can live in our fast-paced, tech-centered world and still harness the delight of existence and artistic creation without giving away our souls to platforms and vices that are not designed to support mindfulness and abundance. It's important that we question technology, but that doesn't mean we have to outright reject it.

Creativity is the medium through which we can metabolize the experience of being alive. It is more than just hobbies or frivolous activities. It is the centerpiece of a life well lived. In a world that profits and benefits from our distraction, it is a radical act to keep creativity at the forefront of our lives. We are here to do so much, and recentering our attention gives us a foundation on which to stand firmly instead of floating on shaky ground.

Throughout this book, I center the part of myself that is an art teacher to help you reconnect with who you truly are and what your Higher Power is calling you to produce. Picture Miss Frizzle meets *Clarissa Explains It All* meets Carrie Bradshaw for an all-in-one weirdo, queer, art freak, teaching everything from improvisational quilting to writing to making books to creating newsletters and beyond. While I am an artist, it is my connection to supporting artists that leads me to this unrelenting desire to regain my proficiency in traversing the rocky topography of attention. Ritual over routine can be a starting point for this.

In almost every self-help nook and cranny, "morning routines" are offered as a remedy to our chaos and a tactic to get us to pick up the newest gadget, planner, or trend. While routines like this can certainly be helpful, I've found much more substantial success with rituals. So in this book, I will not share my routines with you; instead, I will share my magic spells—my sacred actions, the seemingly mundane things that don't immediately move the needle. The ritual of tying my shoes gets me out the door on my walk. The ritual of feeding the dog keeps the dog fed. The ritual of lighting my candles and doing my morning pages keeps my morning grounded. I will share these sacred practices and many more to show you how simple and profound it can be to turn toward ceremony and prayer outside of religious or spiritual doctrine. Morning pages are a practice I have been doing for years, which are three pages of unin-terrupted journaling created by Julia Cameron in her book *The Artist's Way*. I don't have to always do them first thing in the morning, but can shift the practice to whenever I need to pause and brain dump a bit. "Afternoon pages" work just as well for me.

In a world that fragments our attention and sells it back to us in tiny dopamine-soaked hits, turning toward ourselves and our practices is an act of defi-ance against the systems that are built to keep us small. You are here to go inward, to find what is within, to find what wants to pour out of you. Not just for your own selfish reasons, but for the benefit of the people who will experience your creative offerings.

There are so many things vying for your attention—notifications, obligations, social media, the hum of urgency that modern life says is normal. There may be a million things that are worthy of your energy, and when you start reclaiming your attention, you'll likely find that rest flows with more ease and you're better equipped to engage with them all from a healthier space.

But this isn't about becoming more productive or even tapping into inspiration. I want you to find awe, wonder, and belonging in everything you do. In a world that monopolizes our time and attention, we must choose to intentionally carve out more for ourselves. This creativity echoes out into the world, and that is the greatest gift.

I have been teaching my rituals and systems of devo-tion and creativity online since 2017, helping thousands of students and readers cultivate their own creative attention while generating income for themselves through their art. This is something I have managed to do as an artist, through hell and high water, and something that demands one thing and one thing only: attention. You can call it focus, wonder, awe, or timeline collapsing. You could argue that first you need money, safe housing, resources, food, and connection in order to feel safe and free enough to engage intentionally in your creativity. This can be true for many of us. But it's important that we practice piecing back together the fragmented parts of our brains and hearts so we can become devoted to the deep work, not just the glazed-over, rushed work that we have become so accustomed to in the digital age. When we do this work in tandem with procuring our basic needs, we create lasting safety that is in alignment with our deepest values. This is not easy work, but it is worthy work.

When I'm faced with the question of how to pursue creativity in times of survival, I often think of Jean Genet writing in his jail cell, of writers with children and bills and three jobs, of Frida Kahlo and Henri Matisse painting from bed despite their chronic pain, of Leonard Peltier painting for decades as a political prisoner. How did they do what they did under less-than-ideal circumstances? Deep, inward, focused attention is a practice we can nurture and draw from despite our surrounding conditions. Artists like these throughout history have shown us that in all places, times, and environments, people have been able to draw from their deep well of inspiration, hope, and discipline to create beautiful, life-altering works. And I encourage you to find the chosen and blood ancestors and elders who came before you and have done the same. We can't reclaim this sacred aspect of our humanity alone; we must do it in community, both with those who are living and those who have passed.

UNWINDING FROM DISTRACTION

Growing up, my family never went on a fancy vacation to Disney World, Paris, or even across the country. We did something much better: We would pack up the minivan and the dogs, go up to Platte River Campground site 413—about two hours north of our home in Grand Rapids, Michigan—and create our own little world for a few days. I never saw my dad more calm, quiet, and at peace than in that place. It was like an oasis of luxury—grilling corn over the fire, throwing back beers, listening to the radio. It was his personal heaven, and mine too.

My dedication to unwinding my distracted nature is rooted in returning to the level of curiosity and reverence I had as a child at that campground, sitting under a tree in the forest a few hours from my childhood home, unable to put a book down. When I recall those moments, I have no recollection of wondering what other people thought of me or what anyone else was doing, and I certainly wasn't fixated on if I was doing something right or not. I was happy being exactly who I was: a little kid under a tree, both transcending this world through books and being deeply rooted in the forest.

Juxtapose this with our current digital landscape of never-ending podcasts, phone notifications, and social media posts, and it's clear that we have lost our way a bit. The days of getting completely lost in a memoir, fantasy novel, or the deep learning of a nonfiction book have turned into skimming books just long enough to quote them in a newsletter or social media caption. And writing with intention and taking the time to go back and revise it has been replaced with diaristic flows of consciousness.

Luckily, I believe there is a path back to the deep attention we all long for, and I have set out on a disciplined and clumsy journey to find it. Waking up early to write, leaving social media for extended stretches, and deeply healing my relationship to codependency and validation addiction have become continuous touchstones of my recovery process. It is a story of complete defeat and surrender, and also great triumph and joy. Slowly but surely, I have gotten back to that feeling under the tree. I can read again, watch movies, pay attention in a conversation, and make my art with care, solitude, and connection to spirit and people. I had reached a state in my time of disconnection where I didn't think this would ever be possible. I was so far gone from being able to do anything for more than a few minutes at a time without scrolling for a dopamine hit. I imagine you have caught yourself in the same mindless cycles.

In these pages, I won't flood you with prescriptive methods, but I will take you on the slow and trudging journey of how I cultivated and reclaimed my attention. One of the major touch points of this process was leaning into clarity and stepping away from vagueness. I did this by filing seven years of taxes at once and being handed a giant bill from the IRS. I did this by leaving relationships that made my nervous system feel like it was on fire. And I did this by leaving alcohol behind in 2011. Many circumstances of privilege were not stacked in my favor, but I have found a way to rearrange the bricks of attention one by one. To lay down a path of stones that may wobble at times but has found its roots steady in the ground.

The thing about getting sober—from anything, technology included—is that it unleashes a spiritual hunger in you that leaves you dying for something else, searching endlessly through TV shows, sex, or food until there is nothing left to consume and it's just you and god, spirit, the universe, clouds, Mary Magdalene, Group of Drunks, Good Orderly Direction, a doorknob, or whatever you're into that isn't you and your ego. Sick and tired of being sick and tired, I turned to my work. I found boundless enjoyment in writing my weekly newsletter, teaching, and facilitating digital spaces, but the guilt and shame I felt for having the privilege to do that work blocked me from truly absorbing the magic of it all. The gifts I was asked to give the world were being given, but there was a level of discomfort I couldn't quite shake before I started this process. I felt that ease and abundance was beyond my window of tolerance, and I had stretched my capacity to match it.

A quick note: Although I mention it briefly here, I won't go deep into the complexities of food or sex addictions/distractions because they are not my area of expertise. I mention them here because, while I don't identify as someone with disordered eating or a sex addiction, I have had to face them from time to time on my healing journey, so I know they are very real. Regardless of what habits you choose to work with throughout your journey, this book is a place for you to safely engage with them with as little shame, guilt, or judgment as possible. Your distractions, addictions, or compulsive habits may be very different from the examples I use throughout the book, and that's okay; the core work is all the same.

Additionally, in your pursuit of ease and deep inner attention, you will likely feel uncomfortable feelings that may make you feel small or unmotivated. But the thing about feeling like you deserve something is that it doesn't always just appear; you have to act as if it has. Act as if the miracle has occurred or the change has happened. Act as if the things you want are already yours. And with wild gratitude, say thank you for them every day. Out of all the tools I've implemented along the way, a daily gratitude list has been one of the most profound (more on this later).

Social media is the biggest distractor we'll touch on together, and while it gave me access to my career, community, and cultural relevance and reach, healing my relationship with it was one of the best things I've done for myself. The thought of leaving it behind was one of the scariest things I ever faced, which feels both strange yet important to say. I was convinced I was trapped and that I could never escape the hold of the algorithm machine. But by being proactive and believing in myself and my identity outside of an app, I was able to. I continue to build the tools necessary to keep it from taking over my life, even though my connection to the world felt ruptured in doing so. And it is my intention to share these with you so you can do the same.

THE IMPORTANCE OF THIS WORK

For three years, I tried to work on this book, but I could never sit down for more than a few minutes. I was totally blocked by its possibility. It wasn't until I deactivated my social media, left all my other distractions behind, and started the great experiment of regaining my attention that the book started to pour out of me. I committed to waking up at 5:30 am on writing days before the world was awake, blocking websites, and trusting that spirit would guide my fingers and nourish the crops of my writing.

I imagine you might feel some inner hesitancy to leave social media or take a break from your digital world. Maybe it's not social media for you, but rather food, TV, or some other coping strategy that keeps you from fully engaging in your creative passions. Whatever it is that's gripping your attention, I gently invite you to surrender to the journey of this book. With no judgment, see what comes up for you as you read. Let the discomfort, frustration, or urge to distract wash over you like an easy rain. Take what you like and leave the rest.

Technology has given me access to the most beautiful self-employed career as a writer, teacher, and artist. It also stole everything I had under that tree in the campground, and against all odds, I was determined to get it back. Not just for myself, but as part of my commitment to service in my job, my personal life, and my art practice. There are days when the pull of the digital addiction loop and my other vices still feels too strong to conquer, but every day that I focus on my deep work, I am closer to myself and farther from the loop of distraction. I am closer to devoting myself to my work as a commitment to liberation and the radical act of artistry, making sense of the pieces one paint stroke at a time.

Inch by inch, I have found my way back there. Not only to those trees in the campground, but to the essence of true presence. I didn't meditate every day or go on a medicinal plant journey. I didn't get hypnotized or sing chants. I prayed, I stayed grateful, and I finally opened my growing pile of mail. I surrounded myself with other people who were willing to put the same kind of work into their process and practice. I quit obsessing over social media, I stopped being in relationships with people at sure signs of incompatibility, and I started protecting my time and attention fiercely so I could be in the most profound state I know: awe.

In this stage of life, you may be feeling how I used to, like your attention is fractured beyond repair, and this feeling is one to honor. Social media, technology, and all our fixations are designed to keep us from putting them down. It is my hope that my story shows you what is possible on the other side of recovery. Retrieving a sense of self, gratitude, acceptance, and wonder for the world is no easy task. It requires a daily effort of reclaiming attention as your own by designing your days in a way that takes you into a new world of creation and reverence for your practice.

Throughout this book, you will learn how to start trusting the cycles of your life (both internal and external), stop comparing your insides to other people's outsides, and unapologetically commit to routines and practices that fit your specific needs. You will do this through a series of inventories, audits, and journaling exercises. You will become a detective of spirit, looking at the corners of time and energy to see where your attention is going and how to reclaim it. Recovering attention isn't just about paying attention; it's about living a life suitable to your personal preferences, needs, and desires while also freely experimenting and playing. As you uncover your personal truths, you'll come to understand how your energy moves. Some days you'll feel inspired to write, and other days all you'll want to do is watch reality TV. Some weeks you'll feel like socializing and being with others, and other times you'll want to go into deep hermit mode. All of these versions of you are perfectly imperfect and valid.

In the chapters to come, I'll walk you through the various systems I use to navigate my personal rhythms. These systems, namely, the process of putting pen to paper and analyzing how I spent my time and how my attention was cultivated or fractured, have been fine-tuned over the years through my teaching and personal experiments. We'll explore similar practices together. Perhaps some of these techniques will be too new age for you or maybe you'd like to take a practice a step further. No matter how you relate, you can start by just noticing which times of day you have the most energy for which tasks and go with that.

Above all, my aim here is to help you realize that this feeling of disconnection does not have to remain your reality. Through the practices and systems I will share with you, my life has completely transformed. I am no longer overwhelmed and frozen by the world around me, and I can now look at it head on, greet it with my full capacity, or know that I am at a low capacity and need to consume less. I am less afraid of sharing my beliefs, opinions, and joy in public. I am less afraid of messing up and more accepting of my imperfections. I no longer fall into codependent patterns that cause me to give too much of myself to others. I am no longer in the loop of wondering what's wrong with me, why I can't fix myself fast enough, and all the other stories I told myself before I started this process. I am now able to let myself be a clear channel so I can get out of my own way and let everything in—the good, the bad, the scary, the disorienting.

So much is possible. The world is so big and bright beyond the walls of distraction, filled to the brim with art and connection and less isolation. It took me a very long time to get to the point where I was ready to change, and some of those changes happened slowly. When I truly took the leap to divest from unhealthy indulgences, the net of community care and spirit caught me, and I was thrown into a whole new world of deep attention. It is my hope that my story brings you to this turning point much quicker. May this book bring you closer to the awe and hope of your life so you may be of great service to the world. Freedom awaits.

1

WHAT ARE YOU AVOIDING?

If you have opened this book, you're likely struggling to keep your attention on any one thing long enough to see it to its completion. Or perhaps you want to bring more care and intention into your daily actions. You also might want to build better habits, digital hygiene, and energetic sovereignty in your life. This book will help with all of that. However, there are a few missing pieces we need to look at before we can get to the solutions, and the biggest one is uncovering what you are avoiding. I know, I know, it's a big undertaking, and a part of you might want to avoid it. I can relate to that feeling; avoiding clarity was a favorite trick of mine.

For me, the answer was clear for many years without me having to do much deep diving: I was avoiding clarity around my relationship with money, and it was causing a ton of anxiety and fractured attention. At that point of my life, I hadn't filed my taxes in seven years, which also meant no bookkeeping, no setting aside money for taxes, and no budgeting. This left me in a constant state of fear and shame, and it put me in heaps of debt.

At some point in my avoidance the overwhelm became too much, and I felt like I had avoided so much for so long that it didn't really matter anymore. Once I had six figures of debt AND my mortgage, it felt like money wasn't real and I might as well just keep avoiding it. But that wasn't helping, and I was only getting more and more anxious in the process. I certainly had plenty of lows that you'd think would have set me straight, like when the State of California garnished everything in my bank account because my tax payment plan had lapsed. It was a huge wake-up call, but it still took me another year to truly stop compulsively spending and using credit cards in an unhealthy way.

My journey with money is a big part of this book because it was the root of what I was avoiding that led me to a tech addiction and no attention left for writing, reading, or any creative work. It takes what it takes, but part of why I tell my story is so that you'll have a shorter distance to climb to get to the same result—and so that you won't have to be in the middle of something important when you realize you have no money left in your bank account.

The world doesn't set us up to pay attention, and with excessive distractions competing for our energy, like shopping, food, tech, sugar, drugs, and anything else we can get our hands on to numb out, it's no wonder many of us fall into cycles of avoidance. And why wouldn't we want to numb out in a world filled with violence and suffering? I've been there. But as I learned throughout my journey, avoidance really doesn't get us anywhere. True emotional repair and personal freedom comes from letting go of what's holding us back and adding in what makes us feel whole as a human being. When we fill our days with what matters to us, the other things will naturally fade away. For this work to really take hold, we have to change our behavior because what doesn't change will stay the same.

For the most marginalized among us, this change can be especially hard, as you are forced to live in and walk through a world that doesn't see you or respect your lived experience. For my BIPOC, trans, nonbinary, fat, disabled, neurodivergent, and queer kin, I am with you. My experience might not be the same as yours, and in fact, at times, it can be very different. I know what it is like to walk through the world as both the oppressed and the oppressor, toeing the line of privilege in my race and marginalization in my gender and sexuality. Throughout these pages, I will share my own experiences, keeping in mind these intersections. I won't do it perfectly, but I will do the best I know how.

In an effort to help all of us, regardless of our intersections, get to the root of our lack of attention, we will spend some time in this chapter getting really clear on what we are avoiding. And in the chapter that follows, pen to paper, we will make lists, ask ourselves hard questions, and make an honest and specific inventory of everything that stands in the way of our attention and the life we want to live—a life of leisure, rest, purposeful work, relationships with loved ones, creativity, and passion. And also a life of pleasure, deep connection, collaboration, community focus, and determination.

THE ROOT OF AVOIDANCE

For many of us, our avoidance comes from a place of fear and shame. We have emotional triggers—whether from our childhood, adult toxic relationships, harm, abuse, or genetics—that lead us to reach toward things that fray at the seams of our attention before we even realize it. Reaching or grasping for comfort in this way is not necessarily a bad thing, but we can either grasp for things that numb us out, or we can grasp for things that nourish us. I also find that sometimes there is a middle ground.

For example, although you may turn to social media to distract yourself from your emotions or unfavorable life circumstances, you may also save feel-good videos or make a folder of memes to improve your mood. Or perhaps your favorite snack could both soothe negative emotions and help you get back to baseline. It's not that all distractions are automatically good or bad, attention draining or attention giving, but it's important that we consider when our reaching becomes a hindrance. One distraction I personally love as a coping strategy is finding an older television series, like *Sex and the City* or *Friends*, and watching it from beginning to end.

In the winter, this really soothes me and puts me in touch with a cultural phenomenon I might want to know more about. To me, these distractions can fit into the research I do for my weekly newsletter, or they can just be for pure enjoyment. On a similar note, there are other shows that are purely for numbing out and turning the noise of reality down, but I make it a point to watch these less. Distraction as coping mechanism is not a bad thing; it is just something we should keep an eye on.

When we don't feel safe enough to confront our emotional triggers directly, we tend to distract ourselves as a protective mechanism. At some point, these mechanisms may have actually kept us safe from an angry parent, a frightening partner, or a space of violence, but there are also plenty of times when we simply distract ourselves from uncomfortable feelings, often to our detriment. We learn protective measures because they protect us. For example, drinking alcohol used to work very well at calming my nervous system and helping me relax . . . until it didn't. For a while, it was the only way I knew how to quiet my brain. The interesting thing was that getting sober didn't fix my uncomfortable feelings; if anything, it just made them louder. So I had to find new things to reach toward to soothe my spirit, things that helped me relax but also positively fueled me. To this day, I still have to do the work of reconfiguring my coping strategies the longer I live without alcohol or my other harmful distractors.

We also tend to distract ourselves to avoid vulnerability, confrontation, or the discomfort of doing something wrong. Part of why I waited so long to call the IRS was because I didn't want to be in trouble, which in hindsight is a holdover emotion from my childhood. But what I didn't realize was that the problem existed whether I picked up the phone or not, so if I truly wanted to rid myself of the problem, the best thing I could do was pick up the phone and get it over with. The good and bad news is they want their money, so they are willing to work out a payment plan to make that happen. What had built up years of anxiety within me actually only took about thirty minutes of my time and ended up providing so much personal and professional relief.

This is one of the major issues with distractions and avoidance: They keep us from tackling the issues that are in front of us, and the resulting anxiety or internal pressure can effectively keep us from focusing our attention on the things that matter most. Practicing sitting through discomfort is a foundational part of how I healed my relationship with my distractions and how I reclaimed my attention. The discomfort of not having social media or any of your other unhealthy coping strategies is worth the long-term, soul-fulfilling attention you'll be able to cultivate without them. I encourage you to take some time now to get even a little more comfortable with the idea of being uncomfortable. It's tough but rewarding.

THE ROLE OF FEAR IN AVOIDANCE

I find that I am driven by many forms of fear. The fear of success, the fear of failure, the fear of being found out as an imposter. The fear that I'll make too much money and other people won't like me anymore. The fear that I won't make enough money and people won't like me anymore. The fear of being left, the fear of staying too long. The fear of doing it wrong and the fear of doing something so right that I won't have anything left to complain about.

As you can see from this flowing list, the role of fear in avoidance can lead us to both despair and inaction. It is my hope that in working through the chapters of this book, you can be left with a feeling of knowing what to do next despite your fear, and that you won't be tied too deeply to what is right or wrong, but instead to what is true for you.

This fear of doing something wrong, not being good enough, or causing harm to someone we care about can be enough to stop us in our tracks and encourage us to avoid what we know we should do. We might avoid the project, the conversation, the vulnerability. What I've found, though, is that a lot of our fears are unfounded. People want us to try; they want us to stumble and mess up in the beautiful messy way that only we humans can. The fear or uncertainty we may feel in new situations doesn't make us imposters; it makes us weavers of the web.

Fear isn't just psychological; it's biological. Our nervous systems are wired to protect us from perceived threats, and in the absence of real danger, we cannot always distinguish between what is real and what is not. So we freeze, we shut down, we avoid. This is not because we are lazy or uninterested in our work; in fact, it is often the opposite. We can be so passionate that it can morph into perfectionism. Understanding this can help mitigate the shame, creative blocks, or procrastination that come along for the ride and allow us to approach attention with more tenderness and care.

Fear is a powerful emotion that can drive your avoidance patterns beyond what is tolerable or good for you and push you to a place that is not fruitful for your creations. And it's likely that as you work to reclaim your attention, your capacity for discomfort, and your devotion to creative practice by engaging with the techniques I introduce throughout the book, you will be confronted with moments of fear and hesitation. This is very normal, part of the process, and luckily, a pattern that can be broken.

WHAT AVOIDANCE COSTS US

As I get to the halfway point of my favorite walk that boasts a spectacular view of Lake Michigan, I always find myself worried about the dunes and how the sand and cliffside have begun to erode and droop. It is the same fear I have about what I call "creative erosion," when I continuously avoid my creative work despite knowing that it is what brings me to the places I so long to be in—places of inner peace, balance, and self-assuredness. This creative erosion, this falling away of sorts, leaves me feeling disconnected from my purpose and the hobbies and creative practices that serve as my private meditations of warmth, comfort, and repeated action. I imagine you feel similarly when you go long periods of time without free creative expression.

Avoidance through scrolling and obsessive notification-checking fractures our attention and leaves us feeling like we need more and more to fill the void. We tend to feel like we are inextricably tied to the people or apps in our phone, when really we are creating even more fear and doubt within ourselves to tackle the work we know we need to do. The more fractured our attention becomes, the more fearful we subconsciously become of losing ourselves. And this is wise fear because we will indeed lose ourselves if we don't reclaim our ability to face creative acts with bravery, be of service, and be attentive to our own lives.

When our personal truths continue to go unaddressed due to our avoidance and fear, they pile up, costing us time, resources, and the gift of feeling complete and whole. If you feel like you can't keep up with your creative pursuits because of outside circumstances, I get it, I really do. For so long, my debt felt completely insurmountable, my addictions felt unhealable, and everything felt like it was too much to overcome. But once I took an honest audit of what was distracting me and, more importantly, what it was costing me, I was able to clearly see what I needed to quit to regain control of my attention. We'll walk through this process together in chapter 2.

When tasks remain incomplete and you feel the urge to distract yourself from the overwhelm, there are usually a few things that need to shift, some behavioral and some energetic. Energetically you could examine what is affecting you underneath the surface. Are you depleted? Do you need a break? Are you uninspired, disengaged, bored? Behaviorally, you could try breaking a task into smaller steps, setting a timer for ten minutes of focused work, or working outside of the home for a change in scenery.

I've found that even while reclaiming my attention and reducing my time on tech, I still had to find ways to feel complete when I closed my computer. There is always work to be done in our jobs, in our homes, and especially in the world. There is always another self-help book to read, essay to write, email to send, and thing to do to make us feel like we are meeting some sort of standard. But I encourage you to lower the bar. Lower it as far as you can comfortably go and see if that feels more fitting. Perhaps you are side-eyeing me and you feel like your bar is already too low and it's time to raise it. This might be true! But I find that most people have a bar that is set way too high for where they are in the current moment, and it is almost impossible to get over it.

For example, if I am having a low-capacity mental health day or a chronic pain flare-up, I have to be honest with myself about where I am. It can be incredibly easy to keep my bar raised high and grind through the day to complete whatever tasks are on my to-do list, but who does this really serve? Certainly not me. My mental, emotional, and physical well-being all take a hit when I overextend myself. And this has a ripple effect, putting a damper on my ability to engage in the creative activities that actually bring me joy. Lowering my bar, even if it's just for a day, keeps me in check and allows me to intentionally push myself just enough for growth and expansion. I think a lot of us have very high expectations for our work and how we want it to progress, so we tend to fall into these attention-sucking traps of perfectionism, but it's important that we consider our humanness in the midst of our machine-like productivity.

Interrupting these patterns of avoidance can feel like a tall task, but it really comes down to noticing what you are avoiding and why. You can begin by simply getting curious and asking yourself a few simple questions. These initial questions are not meant to provoke guilt, but to open new doorways to your most creative self.

- What consistently pulls your attention away from your creative work and deep desires?
- What distractions have become normalized in your life?
- What does all of this avoidance cost you (e.g., peace of mind, confidence, quality time with others, emotional well-being)?

RECOGNIZING AVOIDANCE PATTERNS

Once you've become aware that your avoidance patterns exist, the next step is to gain clarity around what they look like. The key is to acknowledge when you reach for comfort and why. More often than not, it's the simple feeling of discomfort, a feeling we don't always know the origin of. It can be unease from a dissatisfying job, uncertainty from a challenging friendship, or even general discomfort from being in a body—a flesh vessel that's constantly keeping the score. And yet, with all of this to contend with, it is still possible for you to reach for tools of avoidance less and find ways to reach toward creative acts instead.

You can also start to identify people, places, and spaces that trigger your avoidance. Are there certain people or environments that make you want to tune out or numb yourself more? Perhaps it's a negative family member or friend or a toxic work environment. If it's possible for you to distance yourself from these people and places, that could be a good start in helping you get your footing on your recovery path. But if you are required to be around these people and places, I've found that having something to work on in those environments that isn't my phone can help. I like to knit to keep my mind and body occupied in stressful spaces, but you may prefer to bring along a small notebook, a watercolor set, a crossword puzzle, a sketch pad, or a fidget spinner. Finding new tools to replace harmful distractions to regulate your nervous system is the real win. It isn't about forcing attention with willpower alone, but learning to recognize when you are overwhelmed and cultivating new ways to respond.

Before moving on, pause and reflect on the following questions. Allow them to guide you into awareness rather than judgment.

- What do you tend to reach for when you feel scattered or stuck?

- Do these habits truly promote your inner creativity or are they just there to numb the discomfort?
- What might it feel like to choose something more grounding instead? What is the more centering choice in the long run?

CONNECTING AVOIDANCE AND ATTENTION

These subtle yet chronic attention leaks, like endless scrolling, mindless eating, or compulsive shopping can lead many of us to despair, depression, anxiety, and potentially more heightened mental health symptoms. And perhaps you may find that there are certain parts of you that will always reach for some form of distraction or comfort. Like I mentioned earlier, reaching and grasping are not necessarily bad, but it's important to find more helpful and nourishing activities to reach for. Try your best not to fight yourself, put yourself in a box, or heal yourself with extreme remedies. There are a myriad of tools you can use to redirect your avoidance and reclaim your attention.

For example, I attack my addiction to distraction head-on with a mix of Eastern and Western medicine. I take herbs, prescribed medications, and supplements to soothe my mind, and I also meditate, walk, swim, knit, pray, and commune with my neighbors to soothe my body and spirit. I have a therapist, I get body work done regularly, I see a psychic and a creative coach, and I have a twelve-step sponsor. I do not do this work alone, and I definitely do not put any expectations on myself about what this process should look like. There is a lot of heavy lifting and that takes a lot of support.

My access to and engagement with these tools is greatly limited when my attention is fractured and leaking out everywhere. This is why understanding what we are avoiding is an important first step in reclaiming our energy and channeling it into meaningful projects. Whether you identify as an artist or not doesn't matter in this moment; what matters is that your creative spirit has space to shine through so you can be with both yourself and others.

PREPARING FOR THE AUDIT

In the next chapter, I will introduce you to the attention audit. I want to be very clear here: This exercise is not an inventory for you to beat yourself up, approach with shame and despair, or let your mind fold in on you. This inventory is meant for you to clearly see what is standing on the path before you and what needs to be cleared. The meadow must burn so that it may grow new foliage. Similarly, you must stand before your triggers and what you avoid with confidence, self-compassion, and kindness. Do not judge where you have been, where you are now, or where you are going. You are simply on a fact-finding mission to see what is keeping you from holding on to your sacred attention.

In this process, I encourage you to choose curiosity over judgment. Sometimes facing the self and following the clues is a painful experience. It can make us uneasy to really see how much of our time and energy goes to our addictions and avoidant behaviors, but the rewards of doing so are limitless. If it's helpful, you can complete the audit with another person. This is often a great way to face tasks that are really difficult.

When we confront what we are avoiding, we free up space for creativity at home, in our personal lives, and in our work, which allows us to live in our true expression and share our gifts with the world. Whatever you want to pursue—whether it's organizing a small-town parade, volunteering, joining a local organization focused on an issue that is dear to your heart, or spending more time with your family and friends—I promise you it is possible. There are a few simple steps that can take you there, and if you are willing, I will walk alongside you to figure them out in this book.

This work is about being in right relationship with what matters most to you, and for me, constantly being distracted and wasting my time no longer felt aligned with my deeper intentions. Your shifts might not be major or public. In fact, they may be subtle and quiet. They may even be simple whispers for your attention to come back. Or you may be preparing for a major overhaul.

Together, we will get clear on the deeper purpose of your work to cultivate your inner and outer landscapes of creative attention. More will be revealed in the pages to come, and in these revelations, we will find peace and attunement.

2

THE ATTENTION AUDIT

I developed the attention audit during a particularly challenging phase of life to help me understand where my attention was going so I could begin to reclaim it. It helped me get a clear sense of what avoidance patterns I needed to step away from, what was holding me back, and how I could begin to move forward with intention. It was the scaffolding I used to put the pieces of my mind back together, and now, I would like to share it with you so you can achieve similar results.

Essentially, the attention audit is an inventory system to help you see where your focus is going so you can reclaim your time, energy, and creative capacity. Taking an inventory is a practice I have been doing for years. Not every day or in every season, but it is something I return to often to keep me aware of where my attention is going. Am I obsessed about a friend breakup, how a newsletter performed, or where my money is going to or coming from? Am I fixated on another person's wins or my own losses? Am I aimlessly scrolling on my phone or watching the news nonstop? It's important to take a step back and snap out of autopilot mode to assess how you are spending your time and where you can redirect your attention for a more fulfilling existence.

Attention audits are crucial for any artist who wants to have more focus in their work, any person who wants to bring more vitality into their home, and any worker who wants better separation between on time and off time. It is an entry point to freedom from the bondage of fractured attention. It is the beginning of a new way of seeing. If all you do in this book is the attention audit, you will be a changed person. Being willing to face what is in the way of the life we want to live is truly the hardest part because it requires tackling the shame that comes with recognizing how long we've engaged in the same old behavior or the same old way of life. The attention audit asks us to simply take notice without judgment. What if we saw the world with our eyes wide open instead of staring down at our phone or looking over our shoulder for the next threat?

So again, I encourage you to approach this work with gentleness and curiosity. This is a way for you to uncover your hidden truths and see that they are not something to be scared of, but something to celebrate. You'll uncover who and what benefits from your focus and who or what benefits you. Media companies and tech companies benefit from your focus and attention.

The government benefits from you being overly distracted by the news. While I believe in the power of radical news, I also believe that too much news intake can be another hook for your attention. There is a big difference between being informed and empowered enough to take action and sitting at home afraid of the world around you.

We audit our attention to be more available to action and service, not less. You'll be able to see where the attention leaks are so you can stop them and move forward with your beliefs intact. And by doing all of this, you'll be of more use to your fellow humans and the world.

As you complete your attention audit, you may see areas of life where you aren't nearly as productive as you think you are. I know for me, as I'm working on my computer all day, someone might email me, a breaking story might come through, or I may become distracted by an enticing web page. Before I know it, the sun has gone down, and I've gotten nothing done. This lack of deep work is part of what keeps my attention scattered, but I also recognize that it brings me comfort to work lightly and not feel like I have to be all-in every day. The attention audit will allow you to clarify what is too much for you and what is just the right amount.

FOLLOWING THE THREADS

Distraction often takes an emotional and creative toll on our lives, but as I mentioned before, there's a middle ground here that deserves to be acknowledged. I like to call this "following the threads" or "going down the rabbit hole." Like everything else in this book, this is going to be very personal to you and your experience with creativity and distraction, but perhaps you can relate to my experience.

Twice a week, I host a writing group on Zoom called Landscapes where we have a brief and lively check-in, then write in silence for two hours. The chat is open for anyone who wants to connect, and a lot of times our meetings end up feeling like a cute corner in the library where everyone is whispering to each other. I love to take little breaks in the middle of writing to pop into the chat and take part in whatever conversation is happening, then jump back into my writing. This practice of briefly stepping away is intentional, and it actually supports my writing practice to have little breaks to connect with people.

During my 5:30 am solo writing blocks, however, I run a very strict ship. The night before, I block any websites that could distract me and turn my phone all the way off until after my three hours of writing, meditating, and journaling are done. Sometimes I will take a break from writing to stretch, grab something to read that is relevant to my writing, but during this time, talking to other people or checking in with the outside world is not a part of my process.

These are two very different approaches to my writing practice that I have cultivated over time by honestly auditing my attention and understanding what works best for me. Maybe you love rolling over and checking your text messages first thing in the morning. Maybe you work best in a group or with a podcast on in the background. Only you can know when reaching for comfort fulfills you and when it takes you out of what you want to do. And if you're unclear about what that looks like for you right now, the attention audit will help make it a little clearer.

THE ATTENTION AUDIT

Throughout our time together, we will complete two versions of the attention audit: one right now and one that you will complete over the course of a week as you read this book.

MINI AUDIT

For right now, let's complete what I call the mini audit, which you can do any day at any time to center yourself and bring yourself into reality. I find that this shortened version helps me understand on a ground level what I am turning toward and what I am turning away from depending on the time of day, as this can really influence my mood, my energy levels, and what I might want to consume.

In your journal, reflect on your day and answer the following prompts. Remember to approach this exercise with honesty and as little judgment as you can muster. All you are doing is gathering information that can help you later.

- Where does my attention go in the morning? Where do I want to redirect it moving forward?

- Where does my attention go in the afternoon? Where do I want to redirect it moving forward?

- Where does my attention go in the evening? Where do I want to redirect it moving forward?

Once you've answered these questions, take a moment to read your responses. Notice any patterns that come up, but try your best not to immediately fix them or find solutions. Where does your energy feel most alive? Where does it feel most scattered?

Now, choose one small shift you can experiment with tomorrow—a gentle redirection of your attention in one part of your day. Write it down as a clear intention: "Tomorrow, I will . . ."

Finally, close your journal entry with a sentence of self-encouragement or gratitude for the simple act of paying attention to your patterns. This is not about perfection; it's about noticing, learning, and trying again.

WEEKLY AUDIT

While the mini audit offers a quick snapshot of where your attention is going in a single moment, the weekly audit asks you to zoom out a bit and look at how your time and energy are flowing across the span of a week, which I find to be a nice amount of time to take stock of where my attention is consistently leaking. It builds on the self-awareness you began developing in the mini audit by inviting you to notice recurring patterns: What consistently drains you? What nourished you? What never seems to get done and why?

The weekly audit isn't about optimizing every hour, but instead, learning how to tend to your attention with more clarity, compassion, and intention. You can use any tool you'd like, so if you'd rather use a cute Google Sheets template, Notion dashboard, or sticky notes instead of a journal, feel free to do so.

Step One: Themes and Devotions

On the first page, make a list of the themes or activities you want to explore and place more of your attention on this week. You can take these from your mini audit if needed. Some examples of themes and devotions include: community connection, creative practice, discipline, deep work, leisure, relaxation, pleasure, rituals, cooking, etc.

Next, make a list of why you are devoted to redirecting your attention. Your list could look something like:

- I want to spend more time with my kids
- I want to spend more time on my art
- I want my nervous system to feel more regulated
- I want to be of service
- I want to connect more deeply with others

- I want to read more
- I want to be outside more
- I want more community connection
- I want to move my body more

This themes and devotions list will serve as your guidepost as you complete the rest of the audit. If you find it helpful, you could even hang it on your wall or bathroom mirror as a reminder of why you are doing this and what you are doing it for when you get stuck or notice you're reaching for unhelpful things.

Step Two: Attention Leaks

Now that you're clear on what your end goals are, make a list of the things and activities that are currently taking your attention away from what you would like to be more devoted to. These leaks are synonymous with your distractions or avoidance patterns. While you cannot always plan for them, you probably have a good idea at this point of what some of them are. It's okay if you don't have a super long list right now; more leaks will likely emerge as you regain some of your attention. Your list could look something like:

- Social media
- The news
- Other people's expectations
- Food
- Self-criticism
- Money worries
- Reliving past conversations

- Emails and other notifications
- Sex
- Doomscrolling
- Dating apps
- People-pleasing

Next, make a list of the people, places, and obligations that pull you away from your most meaningful work and devotions. Perhaps you have a friend who's constantly on their phone and this triggers you to also pull out your phone. Or maybe interactions with exes, family members, or awkward strangers pull you from your devotions. Does your work environment or even seemingly fun places like the local bar keep you from fully engaging with your attention? Do you feel like you could be doing something better with your time and attention instead of scrolling on your phone as you walk the dog?

Again, we're just keeping track here. No judgments. You may find that your phone is a big distractor for you. If this is the case, it's okay to find a balance. I understand that our phones sometimes allow us to connect to other humans and the world, but it's important that you identify how this is either bringing you closer to or further away from how you'd like to spend your time, engage in the present moment, and tend to the relationships that are right in front of you.

If it is relaxing for you to play a game on your phone while your kids watch a TV show, you don't need to consider that as an attention leak; instead, it is a tool you're using to make life and parenting manageable. If your family gets together for playdates once a week with another family and you're on your phone the whole time, maybe that's fine too! Maybe all of you need time to just sit next to each other and do nothing! However you choose to unwind is valid. Just be sure you honestly assess how you're spending your time and if it's in alignment with the devotions you previously listed.

Lastly, take a closer look at the specific environments that cause your attention to either leak or thrive. Really pay attention to both.

Attention-draining environments could include:

- Places where alcohol is served if you are sober (this is a big one for me because I tend to want to cling to my phone for some level of safety in these scenarios, even if I don't call or text anyone)
- Someone's home where the TV or news is often on
- Any environment where you don't feel seen, respected, or safe in your body

Attention-renewing environments could include:

- Places where your body feels safe and grounded (like a quiet room, a cozy chair, or a favorite park bench)
- Activities that align with your values and curiosity (like journaling, making art, or tending to your garden)

- Spaces where you feel seen and respected (like with a close friend or in a supportive creative group)

Step Three: Mapping Your Attention

Now that you've tackled one of the more challenging parts of this audit, you have a clear picture of what's holding you back from harnessing your attention in the way you'd like. Now, let's switch gears a bit and create a map of your day. Here, you will drop each of the tasks you do throughout the day into category buckets. Here are some category examples you can use:

- Creative Work
- Admin Tasks or Job
- Housework
- Movement
- Service
- Leisure
- Interruptions

Sorting your tasks in this way will create a clear runway for how you can approach each of them, helping you see through the fog of distraction and piece your priorities into your week. This is a mapping practice. As you go through each category, the imbalances, neglected areas, or distractions that are getting too much airtime will be revealed to you. From there, you can start making more intentional choices around which tasks get your attention and why.

Creative work: This is literally anything you deem creative that fills your creative spirit. This could include cooking, knitting, painting, working on a house project, or anything else that nourishes your creativity.

Admin tasks or job: Whether you work a full-time job, are a part-time freelancer, or are fully self-employed, this is often what I call the slog work. Even if you love your job as much as I do, there are still parts of it that can feel draining, like doing taxes, managing your books, answering emails, setting up meetings, etc.

Housework: This could be tending to children or pets, cleaning, doing laundry, sweeping and vacuuming, or any other household chores. Perhaps gardening goes in creative work, but weeding the garden may go here. Break your tasks up in whatever way makes the most sense to you.

Movement: This is where you get to define the body activities you engage in that support you, like walking, lifting weights, dancing, Pilates, or stretching. I often find that when people first do the attention audit, this is the category that has the fewest activities listed.

Service: This will likely be separate from your job, but if you work in a nonprofit or another organization, you may see some overlap here. This could include joining a local organization, being generous with a neighbor, attending a protest, contributing to a mutual aid fund, or any other ways you serve your local community or the world at large.

Leisure: This is what you do to relax, let loose, and luxuriate in your life. This could include hobbies like bird watching, bingo night at the community center, karaoke, hanging out with friends, watching a movie, going on vacation, or reading a trashy novel—anything that brings you rest and pleasure.

Interruptions: While many may view this word as synonymous with distractions, I like to use this word instead because it's a bit clearer in describing exactly what is happening: you are stopping your work. Where a distraction can sort of sway you away and give you space to trudge back, an interruption stops you in your flow. This can include social media platforms, phone calls, text messages, news alerts, physical pain, car problems, weather events, etc.

As you can see, some interruptions are beyond our control and driven by circumstance. How we respond to these interruptions is not out of our control, though. We have the ability to reroute our brains and start moving in a new direction. This requires building new habits, which can be achieved by looking at these patterns in the face and honestly assessing what we can do to healthily alleviate the discomfort of letting go of some of our unhelpful patterns.

Now that you have categorized your daily tasks, I invite you to start tracking your time as detailed or as loosely as you want for the next seven days. This gives you enough time to account for any variations in your work and life tasks throughout the week so you can notice different interruptions and distractions depending on the day. There's no need to schedule yourself hour by hour; simply track what your week already looks like without too much rearranging. This is a fact-finding mission that will help you become aware of how you manage your time and effort so you can rearrange your tasks so that they fit into your ideal attention map.

For example, I am most easily distracted when I am writing. If even a moment of self-doubt creeps in, I want to check my email, check my newsletter open rate, check my bank account, check . . . anything. "Checking" is a self-soothing act to me. It makes me think I am in control of my situation because not knowing if I am good at writing makes me feel out of control. So it's less about being fatigued from writing and more about my self-judgments surrounding my work. The checking gives a false sense of work, purpose, and control. I am not in control of my writing practice anymore when I start to check those things, though, so I've made it a habit to continue building the muscle of not checking. For me, this looks like using web blockers so I can focus all my attention on what matters most to me, even if I don't feel as confident as I would like.

In this example I have audited:

1. The time of day (morning)
2. The interruption (checking websites)
3. The reason (being afraid my writing sucks)
4. And a solution (app blocker and rebuilding the habit with patience)

As you move through this part of the audit, remember there is no one right way to map your day. Some find it helpful to write this out in a paragraph (like the first example), but I find it very helpful to make a list (like the second example). Choose whatever format feels most natural to you and gets you into reflection mode. The perfection of the form matters less than the clarity it provides. The goal here is not self-critique, but to notice patterns. What is missing from your day? Where does your attention feel the most grounded? Where does your attention scatter like a dandelion in the wind? Mapping the day is a tool of compassionate observation; it is a mirror, not a measuring stick.

For the next week, track as much information as you can. Again, this is purely a fact-finding mission, not a shame-spiral mission. It is a pure investigation of the self. You are creating a map back to yourself, back to a time when you could do a task for more than ten minutes, read a whole chapter of a book, and have a conversation with a friend without interruptions or distractions. Of course, finished projects are not the only way to build self-esteem, but bringing our creative work to a natural ending is part of healing our attention and giving ourselves the opportunity to bring our work to others. My goal here is not to make you feel bad for all the places your attention is scattered, but to get you to see all the places that could be filled with creative, fulfilling actions. You may have more time in your days and weeks than you think. You may also have less time and might need to get creative with how you spend it. Both of these are okay.

Step Four: Attention and Values

Once you have tracked your attention for a week, you can start to look at how your activity matches or does not match your values. This is the point of the attention audit where you start to turn toward the things you actually want to pay attention to rather than the things that have caught your eye out of habit. Ask yourself: How does the way I spend my time coincide with the world I want to build internally, in my home, and in the greater world? In other words, what values do you want to commit to personally, spiritually, politically, and at work? Make a list of these values and separate them into categories that fit your attention audit.

Your values are the guiding principles of your life. These could be honesty, friendship, reciprocity, creativity, justice, or integrity. To identify your values, ask yourself: What do I care about most deeply? What qualities do I want to shape my relationships, my work, and my time? What feels non-negotiable to me, even when life gets messy and complicated? This list does not have to be perfect and final; in fact, it should be a living document that can be edited at any time. This is a starting point for aligning your attention with what really matters to you.

Once you've made these lists, consider putting them somewhere where you can see them every day. For example, writer Nic Antoinette and the fiercely noncompetitive dance class Pony Sweat both have pages on their websites that detail the core values of their businesses. This helps clients, readers, and students know if these spaces are correct for them, as well as keeps them as business owners in a clear contract with the universe about what their values are. Similarly, you can tape your lists to the wall in your office, kitchen, studio, or bedroom to hold yourself accountable and remind yourself of what all this work is for. You could also make a Google Doc and share it among friends, or you could print it out and mail it to people you admire to show them what you are thinking about.

When I reflect on my core values, I find that they often change. A podcast I loved listening to was *Mother Country Radicals*, the story of the Weather Underground, a group of white far-left Marxists in Ann Arbor, Michigan, who worked alongside the Black Panthers and many other organizations in opposition to the US government. This story is important to me because it shows how values are not fixed—they are shaped by context, by history, by who we are accountable to. The Weather Underground made choices that were flawed and imperfect, yet they were also animated by a deep urgency to resist injustice and to take risks in solidarity with others. Listening to their story pushes me to consider what it means to act on my beliefs, to recognize when values must shift in response to the world, and to remain open to transformation rather than clinging to a rigid idea of who I am or what I stand for.

In the last few years, I have even become more radicalized by my anarchist and anti-Zionist Jewish friends who have been organizing for a free Palestine. I have taken to my newsletter platform to share my values of solidarity, liberation, and anti-colonialism, and in that space I can speak honestly about what is happening and how it intersects with my own beliefs. Having a public container like this where I can share my core values helps me not only stick to them, but keeps my attention sharp and to the point. I have become more dedicated to listening to the news and talking with friends and comrades who have been dedicated to the work of an independent and sovereign Palestine for much longer than I have.

Speaking publicly from and about my values isn't always easy, and it comes with a lot of fear of being misunderstood, saying the wrong thing, and losing readers and collaborators. But aligning my attention and actions with my values allows me to open myself up in new ways. Practicing attention is not just about what we do in private; it is about how we live our values out loud, especially when it is uncomfortable.

In moments of political and spiritual reckoning, attention becomes an active, rather than passive, form of devotion. It's the kind that asks us to listen deeply, name what we see, and stay rooted in integrity. Sharing your beliefs is an act of coherence. It keeps your values and attention interwoven.

Perhaps your values do not feel so heavy or warrant such a public expression. There is much pain and suffering happening in our cities, states, and countries, but you do not need to be as radical as I am. There is a time, a place, and appropriate ways for each of us to speak up that align with our values. However you decide to show up in the world, it's important that you continue to check in with your level of privilege and platform. For example, as a white person with thousands of newsletter readers, I am mindful of the responsibility I have in shaping conversation and community.

I sometimes alienate readers and many unsubscribe when they feel I am too far to the left. This serves as a good example that we cannot please everyone. Our values may very well be in conflict with those we love or those we want to connect with, and this is okay. You will find your people. In becoming more vocal about what is important to me, I continue to find a community of activists, movement workers, and comrades who have the same vision of the world as I do, one where everyone is free to move about with ease and care, where no one is excluded because of their race or class.

Step Five: Redirecting Attention: Design a Week

In this final step of your attention audit, I invite you to get curious about how you would like to track your time, action, and energy moving forward. What worked very well for me and a lot of my clients was experimenting with time blocks and designated focus hours to practice redirecting your attention.

Whether you work a nine-to-five or are completely self-employed, intentionally designing your week will allow you to see where you can fold in more attention-stretching activities and reduce old habits that bring you out of the present moment. Again, use this part of the audit as an experiment, a fact-finding mission. This is not an opportunity to judge yourself, your parenting, your dog-rearing skills, or anything else that jumps out at you. This is simply a time to find out what hours of the day work best for certain tasks. I find this to be one of the key components of my whole life.

For example, I noticed that when I booked one-on-one calls with clients after 4:00 pm, I felt drained, mentally fatigued, and unable to fully focus. At first, I felt like something was wrong with me, but in reality, I had been up working since 5:30 am, and by that time, I didn't have any attention left in me to give to someone else. I encourage you to analyze your days from this lens, recognizing when you feel the most energized to complete the tasks that mean the most to you.

If you are working under a boss or project manager and don't have the luxury of being totally flexible with your schedule, find small ways to rearrange your tasks to better suit your attention needs. For example, if you find that your mind is at its sharpest in the afternoon, perhaps you can take client calls then and use the morning to focus on admin work to ease yourself into the day.

I encourage you to map out your week like this and dedicate some chunks of time for specific projects.

Try not to let any hour go unplanned, even if the hour is marked "unplanned hour to do what I want." Be creative here and schedule in time to freewrite, paint, cook, eat, hydrate, and move your body.

If you would like, consider starting a digital detox during this time to double down on your intentional attention practice. You could take the week off of social media, remove the email app from your phone, leave your phone in another room at bedtime, or commit to no computer work after 5:00 pm. Consider this as a way to give yourself assignments to regain your attention and reclaim more time and life, not rules to keep distractions away or take something from yourself.

During your attention audit week, you could also build rituals into your morning and night routines, such as journaling, praying, reading a daily reflection book or novel, writing letters, meditating, or any other activity that brings you into deeper relationship to yourself so you may be of better service to others.

Now, if you're anything like me, you love a good spreadsheet or chart to help you keep track of all this data. If this sounds like you, feel free to enter everything into a spreadsheet, pie chart, or graph of some sort so you can clearly see how much time you typically spend on your phone or computer versus how much time you typically spend on your creative work or hobbies.

As you can see, every step of the attention audit brings you a little closer to your why and helps you be more present with yourself and others and more generous with your time, resources, and spirit. Although the beginning of this exercise may have felt overly self-indulgent, it's vitally important that you crack some of these codes so you can live the life you really want to live—one of great vitality, generosity, and aliveness. This is a week where you can really begin to see where deep work can emerge, both the internal work that is required for cosmic shifts and the work that our creative practice asks of us.

ATTENTION AS AN ART FORM

Attention is, in and of itself, a creative act. It is both born of and requires creativity to begin reclaiming it. It is our sacred tomb of knowing, where we find the answers to what matters most to us and bring them forth. Redirecting your attention will be an ongoing creative process. I promise you I didn't do one attention audit and suddenly know everything about how I wanted to spend my time. This will likely be lifelong work in preventing systems of oppression and forms of technological deception from bringing us to our knees in isolation and despair. We must work both alone and in community to reclaim the parts of ourselves that birth creative acts into the world, whether it is quietly in our homes or loudly in the streets. The time is now.

One recommendation I have is doing this with one or more people. You could start an official The Practice of Attention Book Club, where you read the book together over the course of a week or two, then spend a week doing the attention audit together. This way, it doesn't have to feel so lonely. You could also hop on a call with a friend and design your attention audit week side by side so you can check in and hold each other accountable.

In the next chapter, we'll step out of our personal day-to-day rhythms and look more closely at the digital environments we move through—often unconsciously and compulsively. These spaces are designed to capture and keep our attention, feed on it, and give it back to us in ways that can be addictive and disorienting. If this chapter was about noticing where your attention naturally flows, the next is about noticing where it's being siphoned away—and what might be possible if you reclaim even a small piece of it for yourself.

3

DIGITAL SPACE

Social media is a web, a portal, and an altar where we can speak our truth into the world for fun, service, and self-promotion. It is a place where we can craft a quilt of our most beloved creations and devotions. Although I've talked quite a bit so far about the ills of too much tech time, internet time and social media are not all bad. I started using Instagram in 2012 for my first business, Have Company. I had just gotten my first smartphone, opened up shop in a vintage camper, and filled it with zines, rag rugs, ceramics, and woodwork made by my community members. Instagram was an instant portal to success. It was the way I reached people, made sales, and made sense of what I was doing.

I don't mince words when I say that access to the internet is what I used to build an entire career. It was my entry point for everything creative, and it was my preferred medium for sharing my joy, my art, my findings, and my sorrow with the world. I shared everything from my shop and art gallery, my dancing, my sobriety, my marriage, and my divorce, to my artist residency, my podcast, and everything in between. I used it to share my queer awakening, my ex-husband teaching me to skateboard, and my adventures in both traditional and self-publishing.

In the early days, social media offered me a level of trust and confidence, both in myself and from others. People would see how many followers I had or who was following me and feel comfortable enough to join my artist residency at Have Company, a little apartment behind my shop on the Avenue for the Arts. I used my profile to document everything we did there, from weaving classes and fermentation workshops to our weekly ritual field trip to the beach every Monday, no matter the weather. By choosing to live in Michigan, and later, small rural towns across the country, it felt like I could access the resources and art communities of big cities without having to be there.

In the midst of all of its complexities, technology offers us the beautiful gift of connection. So much about the modern world isolates us from each other, and I found that social media was a way for me to connect with other artists who had the same interests and level of rigor as me, even if we weren't in the same geographical location. I was able to live a fulfilled life wherever I wanted because I was able to connect with peers all around the world.

This is why this chapter is not about condemning technology. Instead, it is about noticing patterns. I invite you to begin observing your relationship to connection and disconnection. How has your digital space both served you and taken something from you? What tools have helped you find creative kinship? Where have those same tools started to fray the edges of your attention, energy, or self-trust?

As we move throughout this chapter, we'll explore what happens when a once vital source of technology becomes too entangled in our daily lives—and how we might begin to untangle it.

WHEN MY SOCIAL MEDIA USAGE TOOK A TURN

In 2015, I wrote *How to Not Always Be Working* as a small, ten-page, self-published zine on my typewriter in the big front window of Have Company. The fact that it would later be in an art supply store and picked up by my first book agent is one of my favorite stories of fate and trusting the process. I never went searching for a book deal. I just did my work, got it to the places it needed to be, and the right people found it. This thread of trust—in myself and my community—continues today and is a touchstone of how I bring my attention back when it wavers.

At the time I wrote that book, I was married and constantly on my phone. Have Company had gained a small amount of internet popularity, and the dopamine hits of Instagram likes started to roll in. I had also started Personal Practice, my dance Instagram account, during this time, which had its own moment of virality. I loved my job as a facilitator and artist and couldn't believe that was what I got to do with my life, but I also believe this was the beginning of a year-long episode of mania that was absolutely intertwined with my phone usage.

In general, I cared little about what my partner thought about my choices. I had stopped being an active participant in household chores and duties, and I had started neglecting my relationship and recovery. Of course, Instagram did not cause my divorce and personal downfall—my mental health was a huge part of our disconnection—but I do think my use of it provided me with a way to become completely consumed by workaholism and distract myself from my real life and choices.

Workaholism and social media intersect in this way because while marketing is absolutely part of work, as is research, the scroll becomes a very fuzzy, in-between space that can trick you into thinking you are being productive when really you're dissociating. I believe social media has led many of us to confuse deep and meaningful work with the fast-paced posts of Instagram. These are different things, and the more we focus on our deep and enriching work outside of our phones, the more our posts will matter in the ecosystem as a whole.

Over the years, I also used Instagram as a place to perform my happiness and relationships and paint a story of my public-facing self that not only looked good to the world, but looked good to me. This level of performance was what allowed me to hide from the truth of what was really happening behind the scenes. While social media can be a great tool in bringing people close together, we must be careful to remain true to our authentic selves, both on and off the screen.

When I consider the quality friendships I've made in my life, especially when I moved to California in 2016, it was always those I met at the post office or the library, those who organically came into my life. It was the other dancer in town who my boyfriend at the time knew. It was the librarian who had a cabin on her property in the eucalyptus grove for me to rent. It was my real life all along that was guiding me to where I needed to be, but I was in a tech-designed trap, thinking that my validity as a person came from an app and who I was on it. It was around this time that my identity online really started to meld into who I was in my real life.

Social media can give us so much in terms of understanding ourselves, our art, and each other—for good and bad. In my case, I found that the more I used social media in this unhealthy way, the more my mania and depression hit their highs and plateaus, and it was both my trigger and what I used to self-medicate. Not so different from alcohol, it worked until it didn't anymore.

In 2018, I self-published a zine called *how a photo and video-sharing social networking service gave me my best friends, true love, a beautiful career, and made me want to die*. It was an essay about everything I have just described and how my addiction to the app made me actually feel like I didn't want to be on Earth anymore.

It took me five more years until I overhauled how I use and don't use the app, which I think gives a clear picture of both its benefits and the level of addiction I faced.

Just before *How to Not Always Be Working* came out, I randomly deactivated my Instagram account one day, and my publisher emailed me immediately, asking me to reinstate it so I could promote the book. I felt like I had no other option, and I also wanted to give the book the life it deserved, so I redownloaded it and logged back in. Looking back, I think the urge to deactivate had more to do with my extreme fear of being witnessed, which we'll dig into later in the book.

So, at the request of my publisher, I used my account to promote my first book in 2018 and then *Getting to Center* in 2020. After *Getting to Center* came out, I could no longer ignore what heavy promotion did to my brain, and I made the decision to deactivate my account once again for four months in early 2021. To prepare, I started a Patreon called the Planetarium Portal, where I wrote an essay a month, had guest artist interviews, and shared link roundups of things I was paying attention to. At the time, I was also sending out my weekly newsletter that included writing and different class and book offerings.

In addition to escaping the mental load, I had also planned to deactivate my account because I wanted to really feel into what it was like to not be there at all, to not exist in the phone box of social media. Through my newsletter, I launched an online class called The World Needs Your Online Class, and it was my most successful online course launch I had ever had. In that moment, in 2021, I could have taken this as a sign to truly make the jump, to leap off the edge and never look back. But my fear and the perceived benefits of Instagram remained, so I stayed.

During my time away from the platform, not only did I have a successful launch, but I learned to ski, quilted more, spent a ton of time in the woods, and started to read again. Before I knew it, my four months were up, and I wanted to log back in for the greatest validation post of them all: my ten-year sober anniversary. I had planned to return on that day as a celebration with my followers, with whom I had shared so much of my sobriety, and because the date felt in alignment. But this time, I wanted to approach my social media usage differently.

After my return to Instagram, I made some rules for myself, and this is really where I began to notice the parallels between my attempts at getting sober from alcohol and my lingering social media addiction. According to my rules, I would only post on Tuesdays and Thursdays. I would hand my password over to my assistant in order to post and check the comments on my browser, then immediately log out. After a bit, I would post, then let myself stay on for thirty minutes, then log off. And at least once a month, I would delete the app from my phone (I would almost always redown-load it within an hour).

Obviously, these tricks didn't work, so one day I made the announcement that I was leaving forever. I felt nervous saying "forever," knowing there might be other big projects that appeared in my life that I would want to use the app for. But my business model does not require me to post, so I didn't feel the pressure to constantly be "on."

In the process of writing this book, and more importantly—reading it back to myself—I made the decision to permanently delete my Instagram account with over 80k followers and the fancy blue check mark. For now, I am free of the comparison, the doom scrolling, and the constant back and forth between the news, promotional content, and reels. I am free of creating posts and wondering how they'll land. I am free of being witnessed in a non-nuanced space. I am free of the addiction of looking for myself online when I am right here.

As you can see, my experiments with social media took place over many years as I tried different tricks in hopes of getting new results and the freedom I longed for without letting it go. But the truth was I needed to build a business and a way of life as an artist without it, and this is something I feel passionate about sharing with other artists and entrepreneurs. As I mentioned before, these platforms have the capability to enhance our careers, relationships, and creative pursuits, but when we rely on these systems for our creative spark and livelihood, we will be doomed. They subtly control our behavior, own our information, and while they may have originally catered to us as users because we were building their reputation, it's safe to say they no longer care about our well-being.

I have found, though, like with any addiction, being without social media doesn't automatically solve the attention problem. Spoiler alert: Quitting Instagram or any other habit just leaves you with another void to fill. Once the app is deleted and the space is cleared in your life, there is so much work to do to regain your attention, and this can be done by cultivating your creative spirit, healing your nervous system, and recognizing your version of god in everything.

Once I took my attention back and got comfortable with all of myself—the messy parts included—I was able to feel into the new parts of being alive, the parts that are really uncomfortable but worth excavating. You might not need to leave social media forever or switch to a flip phone tomorrow, but it's important that you reflect on how you interact with these modalities, how you let them affect your most sacred commodity—your time—and carve new pathways for yourself accordingly. Carving these paths isn't easy, but I will walk you through how I've done it and how I'm currently doing it for a more generative future.

UNDERSTANDING THE HOOK OF DIGITAL DISTRACTIONS

It is so important that you know, dear reader, that you are not hooked on social media because you are weak. You are hooked because of the meticulous design of these apps. These platforms were designed to make you think that you must be informed every minute of the day, and the only way to do so is through their app. The promise of virality, of being discovered, of having your life totally changed has kept many of us endlessly engaging and posting online.

The apps ask, "What if your life could change right in front of your eyes?" And for many, this is an incredibly enticing possibility. But my question for you is: What if you looked up and it was already changing? What if the change you're looking for is inside you and all around you—in the books, the people, and the experiences you surround yourself with?

I get defensive sometimes when people equate wanting to be online less to wanting to be less informed. For me, it has been quite the contrary. Without the constant fatigue that comes from media and screen addiction, I have a much wider capacity to take in current events, act accordingly, and put myself in a place of meaningful service. I found that being on social media created an urgent reaction to world events and interpersonal needs within me, but now I have the time and space to take in all the information I need and present that information through my writing in a way that is actually in alignment.

But this, too, is by design. Social media is made to make us feel like everything is urgent. I refuse this urgency, and I encourage you to do the same. Thoughtful, well-organized, and focused actions against our common oppressor are needed now more than ever, and while the quick spreading of information on social media can help us come together, this is also one of its downfalls. I have friends who work diligently to disseminate news quickly on social platforms to keep our community tapped in and informed on what to do next. I recognize, though, that this is not my job, and I no longer feel sheepish about that in the way I once did. I know now that my role is to be a planetary being and to report back what I find in my newsletter every Monday. The other days of the week, I am taking time to listen to the news and read about current events in waves. I've found that accepting and honoring my silence in the chorus is just as valuable and allows others to come forward and speak up too.

In addition to the way social media platforms breed a sense of urgency and FOMO, the algorithms also track our behaviors. The documentary *The Social Dilemma* showed just how pervasive this system is and how deep it's designed to get into our psyche. As we've come to learn through our personal experiences, these algorithms listen to who we text, gather information on what we shop for online, and analyze how long we hover over certain reels. We have essentially been fed an algorithm that is so smart, it knows we won't ever want to put it down. But if you're anything like me, the less you put down the apps, the more discomfort you feel within yourself, and the more discomfort you feel, the more you feel the need to self-soothe with more scrolling, shopping, or posting.

Our digital space certainly has its hooks in us these days, and while I advocate for spending less time on apps, I like to honor both sides of it. Staying informed is important. Connecting creatively is important. Finding beautiful objects we want to adorn our bodies and homes with is important. But it's also important to take care of yourself, acknowledge how these platforms are affecting your mental well-being, and adjust your actions. If being on social media as much as you are now isn't working for you anymore, I am happy to say that there are ways you can still access its benefits while making yourself a priority.

THE ILLUSION OF CONNECTION

In the digital realm, we are promised that we will be able to keep in touch with loved ones, have a way to share our work, and be able to build a place to circulate information. But the question stands: At what cost? And does the use of social media actually nurture the relationships we are looking to cultivate and maintain?

I cannot doubt the many amazing relationships I have made on social media and other digital platforms. It's how an ex-girlfriend originally slipped into my DMs, it's how I've gotten jobs, and it's how some of my current best friends first saw me and decided to be my friend. This is obviously a wonderful thing, but it's not the only way to build connection in the twenty-first century. Because so many of us use social media in this way, we forget about the ultimate digital landing page: the personal website. This is yet another place for you to let yourself shine, create real community and connection, and share your values, your work, or whatever else feels relevant. Curating a website as a form of world-building is an option to grow your creative practice and business off social media.

While I am living proof that real connections can happen on digital platforms, a question I asked myself when I left was, "Do I have enough, and if not, why do I think I need more?" When I answered honestly,

I realized I had built up so many beautiful relationships, and I had an overwhelming feeling that, yes, I had enough—enough friends, enough collaborators, and enough connections. Now, this didn't mean I was against meeting new people. Each person I know and love will inevitably lead me to more community members when we go to events together, visit each other, organically introduce new friends to each other, and so on. The people will certainly keep coming and rippling out. But I argue that you do not need social media to make new friends or connections; the real world can do this for you.

The first time I left social media, I made a spreadsheet of everyone I didn't want to lose touch with and invited them to subscribe to my newsletter so I could still reach my most dedicated followers and real connections. When I left social media for the last time, I did not do this because leaving no longer felt like such a big deal. There are little moments where I wish I knew what certain people were up to, but ultimately, this feeling passes pretty quickly, and I assure myself that if I actually wanted to know, I would have found a way to do so before I left.

Another way social media produces illusions of connection is by incentivizing its users to project a "perfect" life into the world, creating a space where we feel the need to compare ourselves to others. This is no way to live, and we must find ways to detach from the compare-and-despair game of social media. This can easily make us feel unwarranted jealousy, envy, or even just plain annoyance that someone has what we don't or looks how we wish we did. These fabricated high-light reels effectively pull us away from our lives and purpose and keep us stuck in a loop of self-pessimism.

Digital distractions keep us disconnected from our true selves, and this is ultimately what Big Tech wants—for us to continue to consume both media and material goods and line their pockets. Executives at tech companies are not sitting around in their offices trying to figure out how we can connect more deeply with our families. They want to know how they can get us on the app, how long they can keep us on it, and how they can get us to spend more money. Period. That's the gig, that's the job, that's the setup.

While these platforms were originally marketed as tools to help us connect more with one another, this is no longer the case, and many of us are not actually cultivating real relationships with others. We have simply fallen into the Big Tech trap, and our whole being is paying the price.

CONSTANTLY CONNECTED

I've spoken at length so far about the benefits of connection and real relationships—and how intentional social media use can aid us in that—but there's another side to this that's worth speaking about. In fact, being constantly connected brought me to my knees in burnout. At the height of my digital addiction, I was communicating with dozens of people a day over social media, through my newsletter, and via email. This left so little time for my close family and friends and community members. I was always on, and it was slowly killing me. The depth of our engagement with the world whittles away to almost nothing as our attention becomes more and more fractured, leaving us without the faculties to be able to listen, respond with empathy, or focus on an important conversation.

The people we are so desperately trying to impress or stay close to online only know our projected selves, not our deep internal insides. Our brains are simply not designed for this much cognitive overload, and we are forced to reckon with this as we deal with the consequences. I find that, for myself, the more overstimulated I am—specifically by a symphony of voices that are not my own—the less I am able to hear my own thoughts. I can no longer tap into my desires and patience. I have a diminished capacity for deep thought, focused work, conflict resolution, and empathy.

Think about it: When you open a social media app, you are immediately opening your energetic field to millions of people. Long gone are the days when the algorithm only shows you posts from people you follow. Now you can see anything, and a lot of times, you do! A company selling bags, children dying in a genocide, your high school boyfriend's kid doing a TikTok dance, political propaganda, someone promoting their online class or book, more death, more suffering, a puppy. All of these posts elicit many different emotional reactions in less than one minute. So even if you feel like you are tracking your screen time well and you're only giving yourself ten minutes on social media a day, imagine what you're being inundated with in that time.

This is the root of our collective inability to focus on one thing for any stretch of time, whether that's reading a book, having a long conversation, cooking a meal, or doing the many other things that are inherently good for us. And with the rise in short-form media, this is only getting worse. Now, I want to be clear again: There are always many factors in place. I myself have ADHD, have divested from social media platforms, and *still* have so many things I must do to keep my attention focused and sacred. The rest of this book is dedicated to those practices.

It can be hard to swallow the truth that "being on" and constantly connected can create such an emotional toll on us, but if you have opened this book, I imagine you may already be feeling it. You may be feeling the many distractions, interruptions, and addictions of your life monopolizing your attention in a way that feels impossible to get back. I promise it is possible to restore it and find a way forward. Some possibilities include detoxing from digital spaces, taking a long break, or quitting them altogether. In the next chapter, I will walk you through some of the different methods you can take to approach your digital spaces from a place that feels most nurturing for your attention.

4

DIGITAL DETOX

The idea of a digital detox can be extremely overwhelming at first, mainly for the reasons we've discussed so far. We don't want to be disconnected from friends, community members, or public figures, and we don't want to be uninformed on the latest news or trends—and rightfully so. But consider this: There are people in your life who are currently staying connected and informed without any social media presence. Even if you take a break for an hour, a day, or a week, you will find that you will still know what is going on in the world, you will still have a business, you will still have friends, you will still feel connected to those who matter to you most, *and*, in the process, your attention will slowly but surely return.

A digital detox doesn't have to be extreme or all-or-nothing. You have free rein to make it as long or short as you want and give yourself any rules to properly recalibrate. If you want to complete this along with your attention audit, you are more than welcome to, as long as you stay committed to the core principle of not judging yourself. Like the attention audit, this is simply a fact-finding mission.

TIPS FOR A SUCCESSFUL DETOX

First, you'll want to decide on the length of time for your detox; one day, one week, and one month are common choices for your first time. Next, decide if you will log off completely or deactivate your account. I personally prefer to deactivate because that way I have truly disappeared from the digital space. For Instagram, this will not delete your profile and you can log back in later to reactivate it, but for other platforms, make sure to double-check before doing this. Then, decide if you're going to consume news and, if so, where you will go for that news. You could choose to not consume any news for the entire detox (I promise it'll be there when you get back, and anything pressing will find its way to you through word of mouth), or you could commit to only listening to one news program, like *Democracy Now!*, Monday through Friday, and not checking any other news sources. And finally, decide how you will engage with other forms of media, like TV, podcasts, or audiobooks.

Only you know what is taking your attention, so this is why doing an honest attention audit is necessary to understand what will be worthwhile to include in your detox. For me, I tend to set a rule for no trash TV, but I will watch documentaries, especially if they are about things I am currently researching or thinking about. If it's helpful for you, consider joining or creating a digital detox group or enlisting an accountability buddy to do this with. You could even start a newsletter or a blog to track how you spend your time and what feelings come up in the process.

Remember, a digital detox isn't just about less screen time; it's about reclaiming your time, restoring your attention, and using it to pursue projects and activities that matter to you. So as you prepare for your detox, make a list of the things you are going to do *instead* of what you are detoxing from. Here's an example from a detox I recently did.

What to do instead of looking at social media:

- Knit
- Make a flower essence
- Make a tincture
- Brew some tea
- Run a bath
- Go for a walk
- Call or text a friend

What to do instead of watching TV:

- Watch a documentary
- Read a book
- Meditate

What to do instead of checking the news:

- Stretch or move my body
- Check in on friends
- Be of service or volunteer

Email is usually the hardest part of a digital detox because so many of us use email for work, so while you likely can't take the whole week off of work to abide by your detox rules, you certainly can make some adjustments by taking the email app off your phone (gasp, I know!) and set specific times that you will check email on your computer only.

I also suggest you pick a time to close your computer for the day and turn your phone off for the night. In my book *How to Not Always Be Working*, I suggest getting three things for a digital detox: an alarm clock, a timer, and a camera. These are the three things I often "need" my phone for outside of its natural form of communication. This way, I can sleep with my phone in the other room; if I want to meditate or exercise, I have a timer for that; and if I want to take a photograph of something, I have my camera.

You might use your phone for other things, so be sure to accommodate for yourself as necessary. Perhaps you can purchase an MP3 player for your music or audiobooks, grab a headlamp or a flashlight for a late-night dog walk, or try a good old-fashioned flip phone to talk with friends or family. You could even start a new creative project for thirty days and see what happens when you document it only for yourself with a disposable camera.

Just remember there are ways to replace the things you use your phone for each day. Or better yet, I encourage you to sink into the discomfort of not having access to these conveniences and see what other creative acts take their place.

CLEAN UP YOUR DIGITAL SPACES AND HABITS

Another thing to do right before a digital detox is clean up your digital spaces. Take a look at your inbox and unsubscribe from any email lists—shopping websites, newsletters, forums, etc.—that are no longer relevant or that might distract you or pull you out of your focus flow during this time. A big one for me was unsubscribing from "breaking news" alerts from major newspapers. In hindsight, this wasn't a helpful way for me to get my news, as it perpetuated the urgency culture I was trying to avoid.

During a digital detox, it can also be helpful to have screen-free zones and/or screen-free times. I love a "no phone at bedtime" rule, but I do let myself have my phone in bed for an afternoon nap, to catch up on texts, take a phone call, or let myself tune out for a bit. You might want to have a strict "no phone in the bedroom" rule, and that is perfectly okay. Another rule I sometimes set when I am on a writing deadline is no phone until I have written or journaled for at least an hour, and only then do I turn it on and check text messages. For me, these rules are never fixed—they shift from detox to detox, from one season to the next. I think of them less as commandments and more as ingredients on a menu, something I can select from depending on the project I'm immersed in, the place I'm traveling to, or the energy I have to work with.

Perhaps you'd like to explore going a whole day without screens. Maybe it feels good in the morning to check in and tidy things up, but to go the rest of the day without your phone, TV, or computer. This amount of screen-free time is sure to elicit some emotions, ideas, or thoughts. Pay attention to what comes through creatively and spiritually. How many books want to be pulled off the bookshelf? What kinds of research holes can you go into at the library? What body of water near your home have you not explored yet? In this space, the opportunities for self-discovery are truly endless.

Now, some of these rules could be really anxiety-inducing, especially if this is your first digital detox, so it's up to you to decide what you can withstand and where you can be gentle with yourself. For example, if you get anxious when you're without your phone for two or three hours, perhaps try shortening the time frame to one hour instead, which can allow your nervous system to settle a bit.

As always, make rules that work for you, and be willing to adjust them so you don't get discouraged and quit the process entirely. It's so easy to say, "Welp, not having email on my phone makes me uncomfortable so I'm quitting the whole challenge!" Not so. Maybe you'll feel better by keeping your email on your phone and tracking how much time you spend on it as part of your attention audit. There is always a workaround and a way to reap the benefits of less outside noise.

My relationship and addiction to email was so dire that it led me to temporarily switch from an iPhone to a Wisephone, a Samsung Galaxy with an operating system by the company Techless. It has no email, no web browser, and no social media apps. When I made this switch, my life really changed, and my presence healed in a way I was not expecting. Because I was used to constantly checking and answering emails on my phone, I didn't even realize how often I was working (hint: it was all the time). In my head, I thought, *Oh, I get so few emails* because I would only see one at a time and answer it as soon as I got it, but in reality, I was receiving dozens a day.

One of the first days I had the phone, I went twenty-four hours without looking at my inbox and came back to twenty-five emails. That's when I began to understand the seriousness of my work in a way I hadn't thought of before, and by releasing the hold I had on my inbox, my presence with my friends became immaculate.

The first few times I hung out with friends with my new phone, I was amazed at how present I felt. Knowing that no matter what, no one could contact me by email, just by text or a call, was one of the most freeing feelings of my life. I remember sitting on my friend's couch knitting and thinking, *There is no way for me to work right now.* Usually if my friend got up to go to the bathroom or grab something from the kitchen, I would habitually open the email app and check things out. Not anymore! I was free of that, and that feeling is precisely why I can't recommend it enough. Whether you switch to a basic phone or just take the app off your phone, know there are options you can choose from.

There are also a myriad of app blockers for your phone. One of the best in my opinion is Jomo (joy of missing out!). When using an iPhone, I have a lot of luck using an object called Brick, a small magnetic device you put on a fridge or front door that blocks certain apps until you physically scan the magnetic device again to unblock the apps.

On my computer, I have used the SelfControl app for years. This software allows you to make a list of websites you want to block and for how long. One of my favorite things to do is set the block for up to twenty-four hours so when I wake up in the morning, my email is still unavailable for an hour of work or writing.

If you decide to keep apps on your phone, that's perfectly fine. When you feel the urge to reach for your phone in this case, one of the best things you can do is pause and get really clear on what it is you are actually reaching for. If it's connection, try to redirect your attention to an action that aligns with that. If you are reaching to totally numb out, that's okay! Just be aware of it and maybe set a timer for yourself so you can numb out on social media for ten minutes and then be done. Pauses are a great way to understand what you are really looking for in all your habitual reaching.

I'll be the first to attest that sometimes these kinds of restrictions and detoxes can lead us to bingeing. I am absolutely anti-diet culture when it comes to food, so when it comes to digital detoxes, spending bans, or anything else with "limitations," I always want to be very careful that these don't inadvertently swing us into overuse. The goal is to find habits, methods, and experiments that feel sustainable and bring us into alignment. It will not be helpful to white-knuckle our way through a digital detox just to immediately go back to our old ways when it's over.

That's why in the remainder of this book, I've mapped out exactly how I have shaped my life through hobbies, movement, creativity, research, spiritual practice, and service so I can remain present even after a digital detox is complete. It's important that we always adjust the rules and guardrails of our inner work so we don't bounce back into our old habits.

WEAVING IN MEANINGFUL ACTIVITY

It can be really scary to take a break from social media, screen time, the news, or TV because of the unknown. We don't really know what to reach for instead to soothe ourselves, we don't fully know what emotions or thoughts want to come through, and we might be afraid of just being with ourselves. Be gentle with yourself during this process.

On the surface, it may seem like nothing to put down the phone or log off social media for a while, but in practice, it can feel a lot more difficult, as it allows space for uncomfortable feelings to emerge. I always like to remind my students and readers that I am not a therapist, just a tornado person who has found ways to help them reclaim their attention. I do, however, have a therapist, and I do a lot of this work alongside her. From personal experience, it is incredibly normal to need help navigating the inner workings of reclaiming our attention. A lot can come up! We may have unknowingly been using our phones to mask, hide, or feel safe. They are our self-soothing tool. So when we engage in something like a digital detox, it's important that we move toward other practices and principles that allow us the same sort of soothing in a more sustainable, health-promoting way. Over time, our neural pathways will change, and we will no longer be stuck in these ruts.

In the latter half of this book, I dive into five practices—hobby, movement, creative, research, and spiritual—that set the foundation for replacing behaviors that don't fulfill us with ones that do. Beyond these five practices, I will also talk about getting right with money to support your overall attention, being of service in your business and personal life, and planning your own creative retreat, either at home or away, as a way of completely dedicating yourself to this exploration of self and practice.

Giving yourself time away from screens and constant digital input will give your mind and heart so much room for expansion. You are going to be met with new ideas, new forms of thinking, and new shapes of your work. You also might be met with discomfort and annoyance. This is all part of the process of the great digital detox experiment. This is why one of the practices you will get most familiar with is making space for self-reflection. It could be helpful to have a journal that is just for the detox so you can see exactly what's coming up for you. Each night, as another audit of sorts, you can ask yourself:

- What emotions came up throughout the day that made me want to reach?
- What did I reach for instead?
- Did I break one of my rules today? If so, how did I treat myself in response?

In addition to asking yourself those three questions, each evening you can also write a fact list: here is what happened, here is what I noticed, and here are five things I am grateful for. This small act of attention—naming what you are grateful for—will begin to shift your relationship with time, technology, and self. When we practice gratitude regularly, it recalibrates our focus toward sufficiency rather than scarcity. It has a way of rooting us in the right now, the right here, especially when the digital world has a habit of pulling us into overwhelm and fear.

When I first got sober, I remember people saying they were grateful alcoholics, and I just couldn't believe it. It seemed like being an alcoholic was the worst thing that could have ever happened to me, but after some time I realized that it was the best thing that could have happened to me because it brought me community, fellowship, god, friends, and my ability to apply the principles of sobriety to other areas of my life. Perhaps after completing your digital detox, you'll see how your tech addiction has brought you closer to understanding yourself better as well.

Once your detox is over, I encourage you to continue your self-reflection and to get curious about what you want to implement more permanently and what can be saved for another detox or break. I know some people who take a month off social media once a quarter or twice a year, while others decide to quit completely. The choice is always yours.

What I know to be true for almost everyone, even the people who use social media for work, is we need it less than we think we do. Even if you've cultivated the most lucrative social media feed, you likely don't need to check it every hour. And if you do and you feel trapped in that, this could be a sign that you need to pivot your business boundaries or plan. And that's okay! That's what this is all about: being honest about the kind of life we want and pivoting when our actions and values seem to be out of alignment.

EMBRACE THE SILENCE

The constant chatter of social media, the news, email, TV, and other digital spaces fills us up more than we realize. What you might notice the most in your social media detox is the quiet, the silence, the sheer beauty and spaciousness of your own mind inventing new thoughts and ideas.

When I deactivated social media, I couldn't believe how much I was able to invent. Suddenly, there was so much I wanted to bring forward into the world, and I had so much more room in my brain to formulate new ideas and plans. Instead of watching random people on the internet or being bombarded by ads for things I wanted (or didn't want but would buy anyway), I was able to relax in the quiet and the brilliance of my own mind. The silence grew into its own beautiful form of creation.

When you're so used to having constant background noise in your ears, prolonged silence can feel extremely uncomfortable. It can feel painful to tap into your emotions, and you may feel the urge to resort back to your avoidance patterns. In a digital detox, silence can be loud in its own way, showing us the parts of ourselves that we may have swept under the rug and not tended to. Let this be another call for gentleness, for space, for accepting yourself as you are.

I find that the longer I am away from social media, email apps, and breaking news cycles, the more capacity I have to manage the discomfort of silence. Especially as a white person dedicated to unlearning white supremacy and all systems of oppression, this requires that I am sometimes uncomfortable. I may make mistakes and need gentle corrections, I may need to make amends, and I may be in a situation of misunderstanding. All of these instances require me to get comfortable with discomfort, and a digital detox is a great, gentle way for me to practice this. This is how this work can begin to extend into other areas of life. Today, it's just a digital detox, but tomorrow it can be untangling ourselves from the ills of the oppressive systems we live under.

The silence during your digital detox will likely be loud, but so is the bird song, the hum of the fridge, the patter of the rain on your window. I find with less digital addiction, the orchestra of the world grows louder, and I am met with a safety and a calmness that brings me joy, comfort, and hope for a more connected experience.

BUILDING LONG-TERM HABITS

While a digital detox is important, this book is ultimately dedicated to helping you form long-term practices that will support you for overall better digital habits that allow you to reclaim your attention and creativity. While a detox can certainly show us where our leaks are, it is not a long-term solution. Your job might require you to have email on your phone, you might want to stay on social media, or you may need to subscribe to a newsletter to stay up to date on a topic you're invested in. It's definitely possible to avoid digital spaces altogether, but the most sustainable path forward is healing your relationship with the digital world so you can interact with it in a healthier way.

After your detox is complete, consider creating a new list of rules and containers that fit better as daily habits.

Perhaps you'll decide to keep your "no phone in the bedroom" rule, but allow yourself to check it as soon as you wake up because you know work emails will be coming in. Maybe you'll try waking up a half hour earlier to journal and do morning pages before grabbing your phone.

I've personally found a lot of luck in routine replacing or habit stacking. For instance, when I wake up, I turn on the coffee pot, feed the dog, and sometimes I will allow myself some time to catch up on texts. When that is done, I turn my phone off, let the dog out, and light my writing candle. By the time the coffee is done, the dog is ready to come back inside and go back to sleep while I pour my coffee and sit down to write. I do my first pomodoro writing session before I check my email, but sometimes I let myself glance at my email first, for no longer than ten minutes. I have found that ten minutes is a good amount of time for tech breaks, as it's not long enough to completely break me out of a good working flow.

The pomodoro method has revolutionized how I write, and was a fundamental tool in writing this very book. I set a timer for twenty-five minutes, write without any distractions, and when the timer goes off, I set another timer for five minutes and do whatever I want—check my email, stretch, pet the dog, send a text, drink some water. Once that time is up, I set another timer for twenty-five minutes and do this again. After three sets of these, I take a ten-minute break. I usually have about two hours in me until I have to fully stop and do something else. Sometimes I can go longer, and sometimes I need to go shorter, but breaking my writing time into these twenty-five-minute chunks has significantly changed how I work and my ability to focus.

This routine has taken me a while to cultivate, so keep experimenting to find the long-term habits that keep you less tethered to the screen and more tethered to your life.

THE ONGOING JOURNEY

Of course, one detox will not solve all your tech addiction problems, but it will bring you closer to understanding what needs to shift in your life and give you the time and opportunity to adjust your behaviors so they may be better suited to your creative needs. Over time, you will be able to align your habits with your deeper values and become more aware of what truly matters to you and how to bring more of that to the forefront.

I find that the attention audit and digital detox are the foundations of rebuilding your attention, while the five practices you will explore next are how you can set yourself up for consistent and vibrant healing. You don't have to move to the woods alone and never engage in society again; there is a host of people waiting to meet and greet you in this process. But it's important that you do learn how to live in this digital age with intention and rigor, and with vitality and joy. In this way, you can turn your suffering and mental anguish into art, service, and generosity.

My hope is that, throughout the rest of this book, you find meaningful pursuits in work and living, in the things you've put down and intuitively picked back up. Reclaiming your attention is a lifelong process. Technology and systems are not designed for you to turn away; you must work at this at all costs. It might sound serious, and that's because it is. It is a serious thing to embrace life for what life is, even in its discomfort.

It is my prayer and wish that through the experience of a detox, even one that lasts an hour or a day, you can find the strength to integrate the tools in this book that are designed to make your life easier, more fun, and worth your while. You have a big, beautiful life ahead of you. It may feel like you are too late or too far gone in your digital addictions, but I promise you there is no such thing. There is always an opportunity to return to yourself, and the rest of this book will guide you on how to do just that.

5

HOBBY PRACTICE

Let's begin the process of integrating deeply restorative activities into our schedules by exploring our hobbies. For me, hobbies are unhooked from capitalism, hustle culture, and the grind. When we have hobbies, or activities that are not monetized, we have a better chance of adding more play and fun into our life and giving ourselves something to reach toward that isn't work.

Addressing my inadvertent work addiction played a big role in healing my attention because so often what I wanted to reach for instead of social media was email rather than, say, the pile of knitting next to the couch. It takes time and effort to retrain our brains in this way, but the more hobbies and leisure activities we can lean on, the more spacious our lives become.

Think of all of this as building an ecosystem of creativity. There are branches that may overlap with your job or branches that may be totally separate. Some will weave into family time and some will require solo time. Hobbies demand just as much attention as our jobs, activism, service work, and creative practice, and they could, and probably will be, a creative practice in and of themselves. Placing our attention on activities that are separate from our jobs helps us put a little less pressure on ourselves, which naturally supports our attention at work as well. It took me years to develop real hobbies, ones that I didn't feel the need to publicly share at every turn or take a million photos of.

I like to tell the story of when I sold yarn at my store Have Company. I had been knitting since I was a child, but as I got more serious about it, I thought it would be a good idea to turn my hobby into a money maker. Let's just say I now have great admiration and respect for yarn shop owners. It was a brand I couldn't sell online, so I had to trust that my in-person community would shop for it. I wouldn't necessarily call it a total flop, but it not only didn't add to the business, it completely burned me out. Instead of using knitting to relax when I got home from the shop, I was now busy knitting so I could make samples to show off the yarn that was for sale. I had turned my one sacred hobby into a job, and suddenly I was always working.

This doesn't have to be the case for you. So to help you learn from my mistakes, let's dive into the art of cultivating hobbies that fuel your spirit and feed your community.

CULTIVATING YOUR HOBBIES

We live in a culture that rewards us for constantly doing, but this only leads to excess stress and burnout. So it's important that we take the time to intentionally weave things like taking naps, staring out the window, and watching a funny TV show into our lives. Now, I want to be clear: Our hobbies should not be just another productivity hack or a way to keep ourselves busy when what we really need to do is "shut the whole thing down," as I like to say. If your body is calling for rest, do that! I try to get a nap a few times a week for about twenty minutes, or even two hours sometimes. Especially if I am experiencing depression, this helps me wake up refreshed and with a new outlook on the day. A little restart. Napping can be a hobby.

Hobbies and leisure are a way we can commit to living outside of capitalism, and they can also be a perfect entry point into a trade or gift economy. Your hobbies could include making pot holders or knitting small washcloths, which you can share with others when they buy a new house or have a baby. This is yet another way the reclamation of our attention can be of service to those around us as well.

A digital detox is a great time to lean into your hobbies because you are already spending so much less time online. If you're unsure of what your hobbies and interests are, or if you'd like to cultivate new ones, you can start by visioning and making a list. Ask yourself: What are my current hobbies? What hobbies do I wish to integrate into my life? What would be fun to learn? What themes and devotions do I already find present in my life? What came up for me in the attention audit and digital detox that might support me in building new hobbies? What am I curious about? What am I passionate about? What parts of my life feel neglected or undernourished, and how could a hobby bring me into more alignment?

The answers will, of course, be specific to you, so be honest with where your interests lie and try not to be swayed by other people's hobbies. For example, gardening could be a hobby to one person but to an herbalist, this could remind them too much of their job. However maybe they'll want to grow some plants that are totally separate from their herb garden, making it feel more like a hobby.

My biggest hobbies right now are knitting and reading history books. I am specific about the genre because when I read self-help or financial books, they feel very akin to my work. I am often reading them specifically to write about them in my newsletter or to help me be more proficient at my job, so I try to make sure my hobby books take me to a different place mentally. For other readers, this may be reading fantasy, novels, thrillers, or mysteries. Consider delving into a genre that tells a story that is separate from your career and lights you up with inspiration.

A book that really transformed my life during the writing of this book was *Blood in the Water: The Attica Prison Uprising of 1971 and Its Legacy* by Heather Ann Thompson. This book has nothing to do with my own history per se, or any of my creative practices, and does not have a clear connection to my work outside of my commitment to abolition. It did, however, bring me closer to understanding the history of the prison-industrial complex, radical uprisings, and untold stories, and on top of that, it was a riveting tale of important history. Being a self-led learner of radical histories is a part of how I reclaim my attention. It is a part of how I root into my work as a person of the left and stand in solidarity with those most oppressed. It is how I learn to relate better to the rest of the world as myself and with myself.

Your hobbies can change, so make sure you stay flexible and gentle with yourself. It's very likely that you will be called to turn one of your hobbies into a job or a side hustle! This is completely okay, and it happens a lot. But I encourage you to protect your hobbies as much as you can, and if one does turn into its own small business, do your best to replace it with a new hobby.

If you're having trouble thinking of a new hobby to cultivate, hand crafts, like knitting, crochet, latch-hook, quilting, jewelry making, cross stitching, or embroidery, tend to be delightful ones since you can pick them up while you're doing other things. Other hobbies include:

- Scrapbooking or art journaling
- Woodworking
- Learning to code
- Metalsmithing
- Gardening
- Painting
- Water coloring

- Completing house projects
- Candle-making
- Ceramics
- Dancing
- Long-distance hiking
- Karate
- Tai chi
- Pilates
- Attending classes at your local community center
- Joining an improv group
- Bird-watching
- Playing board games
- Doing puzzles
- Beekeeping
- Drawing
- Horseback riding
- Learning a new language

The list could go on forever! If this isn't enough to spark your creativity, another great way to find a hobby is to think of something you loved doing as a kid. For example, I would spend hours pretending to cast spells and be a witch, and now as an adult, learning tarot and using oracle decks in my spiritual practice has become important to me. So even though this practice is somewhat serious to me now, it offers me an opportunity to play and call upon what nine-year-old Cody was up to alone in their room.

Maybe you loved dogs and cats as a kid, so now you can volunteer at an animal shelter. Maybe you want to learn a new skill, so you take a class online. Maybe you want to deepen your understanding of financial systems, so you take a spreadsheet-building class. Hobbies are endless, and so are the ways you can approach them. One of the most important parts I will encourage over and over is that it is normal and almost preferable that you are not good at a hobby when you begin. Part of trying something new is a deep willingness to fail at it and be messy, with no straight lines.

In my quilting class, we have a phrase "NO RULES NO RULERS" modeled after the classic "NO GODS NO MASTERS." The hope it inspires is miraculous, and people are able to release the traditional rules of quilting so they can feel free to experiment and make mistakes. By cultivating our hobbies and trying new things, we can build our discomfort capacity so when it arises in our day to day lives, we don't feel like we have to run away.

I encourage you to pick one to three hobbies that have as little to do with your job as possible and practice them throughout your digital detox and beyond.

ALWAYS DOING

I want to continue to stress the point that your hobbies should not become another way that you are "always doing something," especially because grief and joy often come through in moments of silence and stillness. Many of our hobbies can increase this needed silence and stillness and bring about the space to allow us to feel our feelings, which widens our capacity to be in states of creative attention and play.

In the modern world, we are taught to prioritize productivity, and because our lives are so short in the scheme of things, it can be easy to want to get as much done as possible to make more money, live more fully, and be the best at whatever it is we do. But what happens when this on-the-go mentality overwhelms us or keeps us feeling stuck? This is one of the things I love so much about hobbies: We get to be bad at them and feel a sense of fulfillment at the same time. Contrary to what capitalism teaches us, we do not always have to be good at what we do, and play invites us to fail in a way where we can safely practice failing and falling. That way, when we do it in our jobs or personal relationships, it doesn't feel like such a dire experience.

When I mess up a row in knitting and decide to keep going anyway, it builds the muscle of not having to fix every mistake I make in my life. Sometimes it's best to take out the row and start again, but sometimes it will stop my momentum and it's better to have one wabi-sabi row in the midst of the other neat ones. The only person who will notice is me, and I have learned to love these unique quirks in a scarf or shawl.

The pressure to always be doing leads to burnout and stress. My hope is that you find new ways to be present that aren't linked to your job or productivity so your attention can float along without so much effort. When we are constantly on the go, we can get so stressed that our attention fades away. It's like working backward. We think the more we do, the better our attention will be, but I argue that the less we do and the more focused we are when we do our work, the better off we will be overall. One thing is for certain: Your nervous system will thank you for taking it slow and just being.

CONNECT WITH THE ATTENTION AUDIT

Overworking and overcommitting to social activities can stifle your creativity and drain your attention, leaving you lacking the time you need to tend to yourself, intimate relationships, or activities that really nourish you. This is why it's important that you integrate hobbies into your life first so you can complete your work in a more seamless way.

Now, putting hobbies and play first might sound like a privilege, and in some ways it is. But I encourage you to try it by even 1 percent. If you have a traditional nine-to-five or any job with a boss, this will likely be hard in some ways. But perhaps you will find some benefit in giving yourself ten minutes to rest, read, or knit on the couch when you come home from work. You could even let your family know that you'll need ten minutes alone in your room to recalibrate from your day. You can begin to put these things first by starting in small increments. Take a look at your attention audit and see where you can weave in some time for hobbies.

I truly believe hobbies are an entry point for breaking the cycle of hyper-productivity and work addiction. Unlike work, hobbies provide an opportunity for you to be totally unattached to the outcome. You could work on an audio project or a podcast that is just for fun and has nothing to do with your job, even if you have another podcast that *does* have something to do with your job.

When I spend my time engaging in a hobby, I find that my mental focus is restored in new ways that echo out to my work and relationships. For example, when I got a phone with no email and turned toward knitting for comfort and creative release, I found myself being more comfortable in intimate social situations instead of compulsively checking my phone and not being fully present. Now, when I hang out with someone, I am all the way there, knitting in hand and no email in sight. Over time, I've become more comfortable with letting my mind rest without constant digital stimulation. This level of presence with others brings me great joy, and the conversations I am now able to have with my friends are deeper than ever.

WEAVING HOBBIES INTO YOUR DAILY LIFE

I imagine you might feel like there is not enough time in the day, and that you are frayed, busy, and filled to the brim with work, family, and other activities. How could you possibly add in one more thing like a hobby? It is my belief, though, that adding in a hobby, even a small one with limited time, can actually expand your time in other places. The key is to find a hobby that purely benefits you. Even if it is a volunteer position that is of great service to the community, try not to pick something to impress someone else. Do something that absolutely lights you up. This inner fulfillment is key in not only helping you cultivate hobbies that make you feel good, but will also encourage you to engage in them often, even when other aspects of life are demanding your attention.

As I mentioned earlier, I love habit stacking and finding ways to easily fit new routines into the old ones I already have. Let's say you are going to try your hand at creative art journaling and you already have a morning pages routine. Consider stacking ten more minutes onto each writing session to play in your art journal. Want even more time? Maybe you could write your morning pages for twenty minutes instead of thirty and add an extra ten to your art journaling practice. Get creative here and see where you can make a hobby easy to indulge in.

Perhaps instead of taking photos on your phone, you can find a cute point-and-shoot film camera to capture moments on the go. You could even experiment with different film types or grab a Polaroid camera and try your hand at double exposure or self-portraits. As you can probably already tell, I am also not one to advise against doubling up on your hobbies. While I understand that multitasking in and of itself can fracture our attention, I love to pair two different tasks with each other, such as listening to an audiobook while I knit, or listening to a podcast while I hike, or watching a documentary while watercoloring. The possibilities are endless! However, think of it as pairing one meditative task with an active task. For example, I wouldn't listen to a podcast while I write a book or watch a movie while I write an important email. I more think of it as pairing one meditative task with an active task. Quilting while I watch a documentary, walking at my standing desk while I update my Notion dashboard, things like that.

So many hobbies actually take up very little time, but they can bring us so much creative expression and expansion. The thing about hobbies, their real trick, is they ask us to pay closer attention to the world and our surroundings. Since they are totally (or mostly) unhooked from our jobs or side hustles, they are an invitation for us to just *be* in the world. A person of and among the people. Side by side, we can indulge in our hobbies and allow them to restore our sanity in a chaotic world.

If it's helpful, you could also set up a specific space in your home for a hobby. I tend to keep knitting materials and projects next to all major sitting areas so I can easily grab them and always have a small project I can throw in my bag. You might want to keep your watercolor materials by the dining room table so they are convenient for you when you want to work. Or maybe you can designate a small corner of a studio or office to a hobby. Make it as easy for yourself as possible. That's what reclaiming your attention is all about. Disengaging from your unhealthy vices is already hard work, so you want to make these fun parts low effort.

Taking the time to interlace them into your daily or weekly routines also helps them become consistent practices. I find that for me, consistency is a path toward focused attention. When I can expect that something is coming, I then know how to prepare for it. So prioritize protecting the time around when you do your hobby and make it a non-negotiable part of your routine. Allow your hobbies to be at the core and center of who you are and keep play, fun, and curiosity at the root of your aliveness. If it's helpful, you can even schedule time on your calendar or to-do list to engage in your hobbies. This also reinforces in your mind that it is just as important as work or your other commitments.

To help you begin making space for your hobbies, here are some journal prompts and a short exercise:

REFLECT

- What hobbies make you feel most alive, curious, or relaxed?

- When, during the day or week, do you feel most open to creative play?

- What obstacles get in the way of making time for these activities? These could be internal or external.

- What might shift if you treated your hobbies with the same importance as your job or appointments?

PRACTICE

In your journal or on a blank piece of paper, sketch out your ideal week. Feel free to check back in with the attention audit if that's helpful. Mark off blocks of time for work, non-negotiable appointments, and responsibilities. There's no need to be a perfectionist here; this is a living document you can revise at any time.

Now, add time for hobbies. The goal is to begin imagining more play and joy and put it into plan and action, rather than leaning on hope and chance. Start small if you need to. Even adding in five minutes here for a nature walk or ten minutes there for a quick painting session is enough.

HOBBIES AND MINDFULNESS

Hobbies offer us a natural bridge to mindfulness, fewer distractions, and heightened, present awareness. I used to boast about how I didn't meditate, how it wasn't a part of my practice, and that it wasn't necessary to be a balanced and well person. But as my relationship with contemplative experiments, seated and walking meditation, and other forms of mindfulness grew, I started seeing how it was a nourishing hobby in and of itself. I started reading more work by Ram Dass, Thich Nhat Hanh, Pema Chödrön (my forever favorite), Allen Ginsberg, and Joanne Kyger. From these studies and my own experience, I now recognize how hobbies are their own form of meditation, their own form of tapping in with the divine. Finding the power to tune in with oneself through meditative acts is another way to sit with the self and to be in the discomfort of silence and bewilderment.

Engaging in hobbies that light us up and align with our values helps relax our minds in a way that screens really can't. We can take this a step further by being intentional as we do certain activities. For example, you can tune in and notice your breath and body while you knit, or you can listen deeply to the sounds of the birds and plants while you garden. Because we are dedicating ourselves to something outside of capitalistic work, we can tap deeper into the intricacies, joy, and pleasures of the world around us.

Meditation and mindfulness, no matter how you practice them, work alongside hobbies to help us heal our attention and create better focus and clarity with our actions and choices. Take some time now to identify the places in your audit where hobbies could be a positive addition to your practices and routines and allow them to restore your fractured attention and heal your mind. It is a radical act to regularly engage in a hobby and prioritize something outside of the grind of our jobs, even if someone tells you it is simple or insignificant. Do not lose this; hold this close.

REFLECT

What forms of mindfulness feel most natural and nourishing to you right now? This might be seated meditation, movement, breathwork, gardening, journaling, or even quiet time spent using your hands—in the dirt, on the pottery wheel, knitting, or cooking.

PRACTICE

Now, make a short list of a few practices you'd like to experiment with, and remember that experiments do not require you to get it right. You are simply seeing what works and what doesn't without judgment. Which practices feel grounding? Which ones feel playful? And most importantly, which ones feel possible?

   If you're having trouble thinking of a mindful hobby, take some time to check in with this reflective mindfulness ritual to get in touch with your current inner state.

- **Where am I?** - Describe your physical setting: What do you hear, see, smell, or feel right now? This is also a great way to unblock yourself before sitting down to write or work.

- **How am I?** - In just a few words, name your current emotional state. No need to judge, fix, or change; you are simply noticing.

- **What have I been paying attention to lately?** - Has your attention felt focused or scattered? What has been absorbing your energy?

- **What do I need today (or this week)?** - This could be rest, connection, movement, silence, creativity, or something else.

- **What's one small act of mindfulness I can commit to?** - Choose one act that feels truly doable and does not stretch your routine beyond your capacity. Lighting a candle, taking three deep breaths, meditating for five minutes, drawing, going outside, etc., are great places to start.

BARRIERS TO MAINTAINING A HOBBY

Before we close out this chapter, it's important that I mention some of the barriers you may encounter when practicing your hobbies. One of the biggest barriers is guilt and shame—the constant noise of shoulds and coulds—"I should be working," "I should be doing something more productive," "I could be helping my partner with something." In this fast-paced modern world, there are always going to be one hundred different things we could be doing at any moment, and as you begin to heal from always being on, resting and leaning into simple pleasures can make you feel like you're sacrificing other important parts of your life.

The best piece of advice I can offer you here is to trust your healing process and know that by carving time out for yourself, you will have the capacity to be more efficient at your job, more attentive in your relationships, and better able to manage the stress of life on Earth. I recognize this is easier said than done, but I'm sharing this advice with you because I have lived it myself.

Because I am always reading something that supports my job, like a self-help or finance book, it was important to me to have a third category of reading material, which is when I started digging into radical histories. At first, I felt guilty about reading something that wasn't directly improving my skill set or knowledge base, but I found that by switching up the genres I read leisurely, I was actually able to focus more intently on my studies and my job because I had given my mind time to rest inside of a hobby.

Although many productivity hacks can be a scam, and while this book is certainly not about how to work more efficiently, I do believe engaging in hobbies can give you the space and mental rest to come back to your work with a fresher mind. It seems backward, I know! But after thirteen years of self-employment, I can attest to its effectiveness. Take breaks, take time for yourself, and it will be worth it ten-fold.

Another barrier you may face in your hobby cultivation is fear. You might fear you don't have enough time to complete the tasks on your to-do list, tend to personal relationships, and indulge in your hobbies. I do not have access to your calendar to know if this is true or not, but I encourage you to keep experimenting and making time when you can. Maybe you can keep a puzzle on the coffee table so you can fiddle with it for three minutes at a time. Or maybe all you have space for is five minutes to sit in a quiet room and close your eyes. Remember, hobbies are deeply personal and limitless, so it's important that you find one that works for you and your schedule.

Start small. You don't have to change everything about your life right now. Continue to see your hobbies as an essential part of your self-care practice and embrace them as a way to better yourself so you may be of better service to the Earth and all living beings. When hobbies become part of the broader framework of your attention, you will see how they are a starting point for the rest of the work you do in this lifetime. When you start with yourself, everything else that ripples out is stronger.

In the following four chapters, I will offer ways you can expand in the categories of movement, creativity, research, and spirituality, which may all be woven into your hobbies or daily life. Before you move forward, I encourage you to cultivate your hobbies if you haven't done so already and commit to indulging in them as often as you can in the next week. Go slow if you need to, but see how you can integrate them into your schedule. It doesn't need to be expensive or time-consuming; hobbies can be and look however you need them to, and you are free to pivot and try new things whenever you feel called to.

May your hobby practice flourish in the light of day and the darkness of night. May it fill you with rest and a newfound sense of restored attention. May it be of great service to you and those it may benefit.

6

MOVEMENT PRACTICE

Now that you've taken the first steps toward reclaiming your attention through the attention audit, a digital detox, and cultivating non-work-related hobbies, the next step is to incorporate some movement into your practice. Finding a movement practice has been an essential part of my own healing and is often actually the hardest part for me. I am a total hermit, a homebody, a work-from-home, cozy, wintertime goblin. In the summer and fall, it is definitely easier for me to access my movement practice, but in the winter into early spring, when snow is blanketing the Earth, I have a hard time getting myself out there and setting up systems that work for me.

Before we dive in too deeply, I want to affirm that every body is different in its capacity and abilities for movement. You might be a wheelchair or scooter user, a cane user, have chronic pain, or mentally it might be difficult to access this part of your practice. Just like any other part of this book, I encourage you to take what works and leave the rest. This chapter is written through the lens of a person with chronic spine pain, but for me movement, more specifically walking and swimming, usually helps my pain, even though it can make it really hard to get started. As we unpack this topic, I encourage you to find a kind of movement that feels best to your body and mind. And if it's helpful, I invite you to consider getting active with others, as this can help you find success if you're someone who struggles to jump-start an activity alone.

BENEFITS OF A MOVEMENT PRACTICE

Movement, in its simplest form, is one antidote to the often-sedentary action of staring at a phone or TV screen. Sometimes simply changing the physical position of your body or standing up or wiggling your body before deciding what to do next is enough to shake up your brain pathways when you're finding it difficult to put the phone down. Movement, no matter how small, stretches the mind just as much as it stretches the body, leading to more ease in work and thought. It is my hope that committing to a movement practice provides greater ease in your life and more acute attention to the things that call to you.

There are infinite forms of movement you could do on your own, in a class or group setting, or one-on-one with a friend or instructor. Many of these forms of movement can be adapted for ability or skill level:

- Pilates
- Dance
- Chair fitness
- Gentle and intuitive stretching
- Yoga
- Tai chi
- Karate
- Running
- Swimming
- Cycling
- Rock climbing
- Zumba
- Trampolining
- Jumping rope

It is easy to forget in this digital age that movement is an essential part of being human. Getting outside for even a little bit each day and moving and strengthening our muscles in an accessible way can lead to less pain, more mobility, and a greater capacity to manage our attention when screen addiction threatens it. While the attention audit works to reveal where we may be fragmented, and the digital detox helps alleviate some of the mental clutter, the practice of moving our bodies actually helps us integrate everything else we will learn in this book and in our lifetimes.

To me, movement is the number one way to integrate research, thoughts, ideas, work, hobbies, creativity, and service. For me, it is the way out of a funk or depressive episode, calming my mania and restoring my sanity when it swings off center. It only takes a few steps onto a trail in the woods for me to feel the spirit of the universe on my back saying, "Yes, yes, this is the way." Movement, like walking, swimming, and Pilates, allows my mind to breathe and my thoughts to rest, and it gives me a chance to totally unplug from all my tasks, including my hobbies, which may also be taking up space in my mind or agenda.

A movement practice for me is not a means to an end necessarily, although I do find sometimes having physical goals can help push me forward. But those goals aren't focused on how my body looks or what size it is; they're about pushing myself to see how many miles I can walk or how many times I can swim in a week. I give myself small assignments and challenges to make it fun. Little movement goals are a great way to get started and monitor your physical progress over time. For example, in the past I have set goals to swim ten times in a month, finish a three-mile trail, and try my hand at an eleven-mile trail in preparation for a longer thru-hike. The goal with this part of attention reclamation is to challenge yourself in the midst of experiencing the meditative benefits. This is also a fun way to include a little gamification, which can help you actually do the things you want to do.

Similar to hobbies, this is another area where habit or activity stacking can come into play. For example, after I have finished my morning writing, my brain often needs a break, and at that time of morning, I have had enough coffee to get myself moving with some Pilates. It helps my chronic pain, improves my mood and outlook for the rest of the day, makes me feel strong, and gets me centered in my body.

Take a look at your attention audit to plan the times of day or week for activities that would work best for you. Maybe your only real free time is the weekends, so you could schedule a hike with a friend every Saturday for a month as an experiment. Live in the city? Maybe you can try a new park or drive to a new neighborhood to walk your dog or meet up with a friend. When I do a city walk, I also like to treat myself to a little "field trip," where I visit a new local bookstore or coffee shop.

Movement allows us to step outside of the constant demands of the world, not so we can tune out forever, but so we may be more attuned to ourselves and therefore have an even wider capacity to take in what is happening around us. As I am writing this, wildfires are raging through Los Angeles, taking the homes of many community members and friends of friends. It feels devastating, and my instinct is to freeze up in response. But from doing this inner work for so long, I quickly realized that this isn't helping anything, and it never has. So, I took a short walk with my dog, and I immediately knew what to do instead: use my newsletter to share resources and hope. This is one of the brilliant aspects of movement; that time connected to nature and our bodies helps us remember our very important role in the web of life.

Sitting in my house, taking in all the news and listening to the impacted peoples' stories did help inform me, but when I go overboard on consuming information, I can't integrate any of it into action or service. I need my movement practice to literally move the information from my head into my heart and stomach so I can truly feel it. I want to live in a middle space, where I am not reacting urgently out of fear nor moving so slowly that I miss a key moment of service. Moving my body helps me intuitively find this middle ground.

When you practice movement regularly, in whatever way feels best, you will start to see how this makes a restorative and consistent shift in your psyche and spirit. You don't need to take a walk every single day to experience the focus-restoring benefits. You can start to reclaim the present moment and your attention in the smallest ways, just as you did in the digital detox.

I rarely, if ever, use the words "exercise" or "fitness" to describe my movement practice, but if someone were to ask me if I like exercising, I would absolutely say no. Historically, exercise is an activity that has blocked my habits and desires, so if you also get uncomfortable at the thought of exercise, whether due to past emotional trauma or injury, I hear you. This is your reminder that you don't have to call your movement "exercise," and the goal of this practice is to create new stories around what movement means and looks like to you. We are not here to push ourselves to exhaustion, but rather to build a sustainable practice that nurtures attention and cultivates mindfulness.

Take a moment now to consider what forms of movement feel accessible, enjoyable, and grounding for you. Maybe it is dancing alone in your kitchen, stretching when you rise in the morning, biking along a trail or to work, or tending to your garden. Walking and swimming are two of my personal favorites that we will explore together in a moment, but they may not resonate with everyone. The invitation here is to find a way of moving that brings you back into your body and closer to yourself and your community.

REFLECT

- What kinds of movement have brought you joy or calm in the past?

- What physical activities feel possible for your body right now?

- Are there movement practices you have been curious about trying (e.g., Pilates, qigong, or ballet)?

- What environments support your desire to move? Indoors or outdoors, alone or with others, structured or free form?

Before moving on to the next sections, I want to acknowledge that not everyone moves through the world on two feet or in the same way I do. For those who use a wheelchair or other mobility aids, the ritual of movement might look like rolling along a familiar path, pausing to feel the breeze, or doing some gentle stretches. For cane users or anyone who tires easily, moving at a slow, mindful pace can offer just as much nourishment as a brisk walk. And for some, simply sitting near a body of water and lifting your arms, rotating your wrists, or swinging a leg back and forth can remind the body of its capacity to reach, float, and rest all at once. However you move, may these sections invite you to find a rhythm that feels kind to your body and steady enough to return to again and again.

WALKING AS A MOVEMENT PRACTICE

Walking is my first entry point to movement that helps me connect with the world and remember that I am a part of the All, to know I am not alone. As activist Rebecca Solnit writes in *Wanderlust*, "Walking is how the body talks to the earth." This movement, this choice, this divine act is both a physical one and a creative one. It is where I get my best ideas and find a way back to myself over and over again. My walking path is not linear; it's its own labyrinth of sorts. I sometimes fall off from my walking practice for long stretches of time and I have to gently return to it. I'm careful not to shame myself in these moments because that defeats the purpose of using movement as an attention-building practice.

This is part of the reason why I disconnect walking, or any movement for that matter, from "exercise." I have a fraught relationship with exercising for the sake of exercising because of the years I spent entrenched in diet culture, where movement was about making my body smaller instead of giving it what it needed. Even now I feel myself resisting movement if it feels punishing or performative. It is much easier for me to trick myself into movement by doing the things I already enjoy, like walking, swimming, Pilates, and dancing.

Walking gives me an opportunity to literally step out of the digital haze and into the real world. It gives me permission to be in my body, which doesn't always feel like a safe place, but I've found that the more I engage in movement in general, the more comfortable I become with embodied experiences. I hope you realize something similar with your movement practice.

REFLECT

Take a moment to gently reflect on your relationship to words like "exercise" and "fitness."

- What memories, feelings, or associations come up when you hear those words?

- Has movement ever felt like an obligation, punishment, or performance? If so, why?

- What would it look like for you to reclaim these words or practices as your own?

- What would it look like to create a movement practice that is intuitive and joyful?

- Are there other words you'd rather use—like movement, motion, play, ritual—that feel more aligned with your body?

The benefits of walking aren't just physical. At the beginning of a walk, I can feel myself bracing for the ideas to come, which sometimes helps stave off the urge to quit. My mind often has a way of working overtime on things that cause initial discomfort, like a new movement practice. "We might as well not even try," a part of me tells my wise self. "We might as well not even try to go on this long hike because we'll just get tired and want to quit." The desire to quit is with me from the first step sometimes, and yet I walk. I walk because I have built up enough evidence to see that when I do so, I have better ideas, better digestion, more kindness, and a deeper connection to the natural world.

While many authors, like Erling Kagge, author of *Walking: One Step at a Time*, explain that walking is a way to be in tune with the rhythms of the world, I would argue that it is also a way to get ideas. Not every walk has to be a magical experience where tree leaves light up your imagination or the clouds inspire you to paint for the first time. Sometimes a walk is just a walk—nothing magical, nothing mysterious, just the act of putting one foot in front of the other. But when we practice this enough times, the mundane act of walking does become magical, in the sense that it gets us in touch with our inherent magic as humans.

I often advocate for walking because it is one of the simplest modes of movement we can engage in. If you feel like this practice is something you can integrate into your life, I encourage you to give it a try. And if walking is not something that feels good or accessible for your body, you can try sitting outside with your feet in the grass, doing gentle shoulder rolls or neck stretches, or simply resting by an open window, letting the air and light remind you that you're part of the living world. Movement is not the only way to arrive at presence; sometimes, intentional stillness is enough.

The sensory experiences that are available in different environments can offer you a new perspective and open your mind to the possibilities, ideas, and thoughts that are waiting to be uncovered in moments of quiet away from the digital landscape. Let's explore some different settings where you can walk to reap these benefits.

TYPES OF WALKS

The Country Road: I live up on a hill, tucked into the woods, surrounded by trees and a big meadow. There aren't any public places in walking distance, so I often choose to take June, my loyal dog companion, for a walk along the road. I use this time to listen to podcasts or audiobooks in my noise-cancelling headphones. I do not consider this a particularly meditative walk as much as an "I need to get me and this dog walking in the elements, and the best way to trick myself into doing that is by listening to something that makes me feel nourished and productive."

You might call this the work walk. The dog walk. The neighborhood walk.

The Trail: The trail is where I go to be one with nature. June runs ahead of me on the dirt trail, taking in the smells and desperately trying to catch a small animal, which she has never done successfully, but her commitment is worthy. I do not listen to music on these walks as I am generally keeping an eye on June and listening for other people or dogs approaching, so I can quickly pop her back on her leash. It is also my opportunity to touch in with god. This is where I find my Higher Power: in the woods, in the quiet, with my dog. It is where I nod at strangers and never remember to bring enough water, but I am always grateful for the way the wind whips.

The City Walk: Whether you live close to nature or not, the city walk can be a wonderful act of meditation. You could choose to listen to the sounds of the people, cars, and hustle and bustle, or you could wear headphones with some ambient music playing as a way to stay in a meditative, calm state without feeling totally disconnected from the planet. A city walk can also be a fun way to explore. Usually if I visit the small city next to my town, I like to pop into shops or go to the library. Little errands make a city walk a bit of an adventure. Maybe you'd like to visit the plant store or browse the flyers at your local bookstore.

You could even window shop and see what ideas spark you. Consider bringing a small notebook to keep tabs on what you discover.

The Training for a Big Hike: This is a beautiful option if you want to push yourself physically and mentally. I find that in my creative projects, having a container to reach a goal is imperative. I think walking can be the same way. While it is a beautiful meditative act on its own, you can also use a tracker or an app like Couch to 5k to gamify your experience.

Whether you decide to train for a 5K walk, a marathon, or a hike, walking long distances can help build your stamina and attention and bring your attention to the forefront. I also love to consume media that gets me closer to a goal. I recommend Nic Antoinette's long-distance hiking memoirs *How to Be Alone* and *What We Owe to Ourselves* as well as Carrot Quinn's *Thru-Hiking Will Break Your Heart*. Reading stories by other queers hitting the trails inspired me to take it on myself.

The Treadmill or Walking Pad: One of the best investments I ever made was a walking pad. While I love to walk outside and find it to be the most meditative movement practice for me, I also enjoy walking on the walking pad at a steady pace while watching a TV show, writing, or listening to an audiobook.

In Julia Cameron's *Walking in This World*, she frames walking as a creative tool to help us generate ideas and tap into the spirit of the universe, a perfect place to download assignments. That is what walking is to me, a place to receive my assignments to bring back to the desk. A place to bring my longing so I can sit in my office or at my dining room table and let the words flow out of me.

Writing is its own strange task, but it puts me in my body in a way that few other things can. Walking itself is not a creative movement in the way dancing is, and it isn't as spiritual for me as swimming. This leaves me with the idea that walking is merely a task that brings me closer to myself and my creative work. It unblocks me with little effort. After only a few steps outside, my worries begin to vanish and my dedication to idea cultivation resumes.

Without urgency, but with steadfast dedication, I do my best to walk every day. Whether it's a thirty-minute lap through the woods behind my house, a forty-minute walk up the country road, or many hours on the trail, my brain functions so much better when I take the time to walk. Walking, even short distances, gives me clarity and purpose. It is the one thing that helps me believe in myself when I am feeling doubtful about my skills and my reasons for being here. Walking keeps me quite literally on the path to self, and when I am aligned with my purpose, I am aligned with generosity, service, and others.

Take a look at your attention audit. Where can you pivot to bridge the gap of the physical and the philosophical? What movement practices can you lean into to reach a little less for distractions and reconnect with your body? This, so often, is the hardest part of the walk for me: disconnecting from distractions, tying my shoes, and getting out the door. Once I am on the trail or walking down the driveway, I already feel so much lighter.

Walking is the way I reconnect to myself, to spirit, and to the natural world. It is the fastest way I have found to come back when I have strayed from myself and am reaching toward distraction. My hope is that you give this restorative practice a try in a way that's accessible to you.

WALKING WITHOUT HEADPHONES

This is where we come to the contemplative, meditative aspect of walking, where we really are one with the world. For this kind of walk, I suggest leaving the dogs at home for a true blue, just you and the natural world, stroll through the woods, along the mountain ridge, in the arroyo in the desert, or whatever quiet, scenic landscape you can get to. Notice I did not say silence, because it is my hope that you can touch into the birdsong, the rustling leaves, and the wind's whispers. May you notice every living thing that emerges along the trail.

As I mentioned earlier, I do not believe that multitasking is a bad thing; in fact, I think it is a great way to honor yourself and know what gets you to do the things you are longing to do. For example, I love wearing headphones as I walk. It allows me to trick myself into feeling like I am doing two things at the same time. Audiobook and walking? Look, I'm reading and getting my steps in at the same time! Podcast and walking? Look, I am learning and growing as a business owner while I move! But there comes a time when we need to deeply tune into ourselves and use meditative movements as a pathway back to our attention. The longer we can go without any outside input—music, books, TV, apps, phone, texts—the more our fractured attention can heal itself and the more we can withstand discomfort and uneasiness. Walking without headphones gives us an opportunity to really be with ourselves as we keep the body moving.

Walking in the quiet is a radical act of presence, especially in a world that constantly demands our attention. By taking this time, you are expanding your capacity to be more efficient, buoyant, and spacious, and this is how you can truly be of service to the world. If you are constantly in intake mode, you won't have enough bandwidth to listen to the horrors of the news and spring into action. You won't have enough energy to call a loved one back or tend to your home. These stretches of movement with no input can give you back hours of the day and equip you with a longer attention span.

The sounds of the leaves, the huff and puff of your breath, the scurrying of the chipmunks—this all becomes a symphony of new attention, a place to bring your prayers, hopes, and ideas. This is when I get the most ideas for my writing, my classes, and my creative containers. It is where god rewards me with the unique assignments I was born to carry out.

Walking or spending time in nature is a way of seeing and observing. What does the tree bark look like today? How has the landscape changed with the season? It's a beautiful task to walk the same trail throughout the year, no matter the weather, and witness what is emerging from the ground—the trilliums and wildflowers, the birds that stay through the winter, and the ones that leave. Notice the details and become the great observer. Seeing the way the rabbit hops, the way the deer runs, the way the snow falls off a branch will give you new points of inspiration for your creative practice. The ordinary becomes a source for the creative output you are working through by regaining your attention.

CREATING A WALKING JOURNAL

A walking journal serves as a bridge between the movement of the body and the movement of the mind, preserving insights for later reflection. With so much inspiration jumping out at you on your walks, recording your observations in a spreadsheet or notebook is a perfect way to track your attention, solidify the insights gained during your journey, and cultivate prompts for your life and work. In your journal, you can capture fleeting ideas, unexpected observations, or even a map of the walk itself—whatever calls out to you.

Years after my uncle died, I found a journal of his that he used to track the deer he was hunting as a conservationist in Wisconsin. In his journal, he simply tracked the facts, but it read like poetry.

October 15, 1989
Weather: Sunny and warm, 58
Time: 6:35
Location: NW Woods
Wind: Calm
Deer: 1 fawn, not w/i range

This is a perfect example of less is more. Just noticing. What did you see? What made itself available to you? You don't have to track your deepest feelings, just note what you noticed. Give it a try and see what comes up. Let what you leave behind be an archive of what you saw in its simplest form.

SWIMMING AS A MOVEMENT PRACTICE

There is this sacred moment right before I plunge myself into a body of water where all noise and thought stop. All I can think about is submerging. There is something in the submerging that frees me of life's ailments—work, chores, other hobbies. I just know the plunge awaits me, and it is time to enter. In this moment, my attention is sharp, fierce, and dedicated to entering the water. Sometimes it is very cold, and sometimes it is very warm, but I like to remind myself that I have never regretted taking a swim, only the ones I haven't taken.

I tie swimming to my attention practice because it helps keep my nervous system at a baseline, and it helps me access a state of adventure. Perhaps swimming isn't your adventure, but you can find another suitable one to replace it with, something that is both thrilling and soothing at the same time. But perhaps you're like me and find solace in water. In the water, I am fully suspended, grounded but also untethered. One with the Earth but also totally separate from the ground, floating through space.

I find that the practice of submerging brings me closer to myself and my visions. It is a key that unlocks what wants to be revealed and brings spaciousness and reverence to the work I do. There is something about the slowness of water, the rush of the waves—its silence and presence—that allows my thoughts to unfurl differently. In the water, time bends and urgency softens. I can't check my phone, I can't send an email, I can't scroll a feed. When I return to the shore or edge of the pool, there is more room inside of me. The breath in my ribs expands laterally, and I luxuriate in my new feeling, as if my body is reborn. My ideas feel less forced and more earned. Swimming becomes not just a movement practice, but a deep listening ritual—one that helps me approach my creative work with more care, clarity, and depth.

Along with the act of swimming itself, I also find tradition to be helpful in setting up patterns for a dip. Every New Year's Day, usually with others, I build a fire on the beach and do a cold plunge. It is a quick way to mark time and remember that the beginning of a new year is here. It's a symbolic way for me to set myself up for the rest of the winter, to be reborn, to be brave and jump in without thought every now and then. I find that this kind of bravery is not only good for my body and mind, but also my everyday tasks, like daunting house-hold chores, my hobbies, or even my walks.

I find that, like walking, there are also different ways to swim, different ways to submerge. Each body of water carries its own energy and mood, and some call to me more than others. When I walk to the creek across the road and dip my toes in, I get a much different experience than when I jump in a pool in a friend's backyard. One is not better than the other; they simply provide different modes of experience. Let's explore some of them together.

TYPES OF SWIMS

The Pool Swim: Pools for me are a chlorinated ritual: contained, familiar, and steady. I can count laps at the gym and see my thoughts as repetitions. I can cannonball off the diving board at a friend's house. The movement can be both meditative and playful, especially with a pool noodle.

The Lake Swim: Lakes hold memories. As freshwater oceans, they are my favorite bodies of water. I live fifteen minutes from Lake Michigan and five minutes from Lake Leelanau. In the summer, I try to go to these lakes as much as I can. The lake can be a cold, dark, mysterious place, inviting stillness. It changes in every season, offering a perfect glimpse into the ever-evolving weather systems. The intimacy of a lake swim feels ancient and alive. I swim here to remember, to return to something true.

The River Swim: I love how a river is always moving, how you never touch the same water twice. A river is a conversation as it pulls and presses. It insists you notice its direction. When we swim in a river, we have less control, which reminds me of how little control I actually have in my life.

The Ocean Swim: What a wild and magical place! The saltwater cave, the majesty, the greatest expanse. Sometimes dangerous, but always inviting us in for a surf or a float. The tides teach surrender, while the waves teach us to loosen up. When I need to be reminded of how small I am and how vast the world is, this is where I go.

The Hot Spring Soak (or Bathtub Session): Basking in the heat of water is a true gift to the nervous system. Minerals, warmth, steam. This is a place of great release. Our bodies may not be in motion, but even the smallest movements here bring peace to the bones.

All of these waters hold me differently, and I imagine your own movement practices can be broken up into different categories like this as well. When I return to the desk, I am changed—more porous, more honest, my boundaries intact. When I swim, I am more willing to follow the current of what is asking to come through.

NEGOTIATING MOVEMENT

Not all movement comes easily. Even the ones we know make us feel better or change us from the inside out can feel impossible to begin. This is especially true when movement has been tangled with shame, ableism, pain, or the pressure to perform. Whether it is walking, stretching, swimming, dancing, or lying on the floor and simply feeling your breath expand into your back, movement requires a sort of willingness to meet yourself where you are. To listen, soften, and stay curious.

When I'm having trouble opening the door of movement, I like to ask myself the following questions:

- What kind of movement feels possible today?
- Am I seeking to feel energized or relaxed? Do I want something structured or spacious?
- What kind of movement would help me to feel good afterward, even if it doesn't feel easy to start?

Negotiating movement means not forcing it to look a certain way. It means not punishing yourself for skipping a day. It means allowing your practice to ebb and flow with your capacity and your needs. It is still sacred when it is inconsistent or small.

Finally, let's talk about the conversations we have in our heads to decide if movement is a good idea or not. There are exactly two times when it is best to move your body: when you want to and when you don't want to. Both require the same number of actions and steps to get yourself out the door, on the treadmill, or on your Pilates mat, so the best way to do this is to make it easy for yourself.

For example, if you decide you want to commit to regular walks, keep your walking shoes out of the closet and by the door. Make sure you can see them. If it is a cold day, make sure your coat, gloves, and hat are also right by the door. If you want to take a movement class, keep your mat by the door too. Keeping everything you need in your bedroom closet offers too many extra steps that prevent you from making it out the door. If you sometimes go out the back door to walk, keep another set of shoes and coat back there if you have them. If you don't have another set, try to stick to going out the same door for your walk each day.

No matter what movement practice you choose, it can provide a gateway to a deeper connection with yourself and others. Cultivating this practice is about making space for new ideas to spark and inviting in stillness that becomes a place where you can ground yourself in clarity, creativity, and delight. Movement is its own practice, but it opens up the paths to creative expansion and more acute attention. How does your movement practice inform everything else you do?

While these creative benefits exist, try not to approach movement from a place of always getting something out of it. It is an act in and of itself. It's about doing the action just to do it. In the way that Thich Nhat Hanh teaches us not to do the dishes to have a clean dish, but to feel the water on our hands and the circular motion of the scrubbing, try to approach movement in the same way: with reverence for the process and not just the outcome.

As movement inspires creativity and leads us back to the present moment, creativity leads us to touch back in with the world and gives us channels for self-expression and service. This is what we'll discuss in the next chapter. But until then, may your movement practice be fun, generative, and calming. May you find what works for you and your body. May you find a practice that expands your mind and your body in equal measure.

7

CREATIVE PRACTICE

Now that we've engaged in movement that allows us to awaken the body and mind, we are yet again one step closer to restoring our attention. In this space of full-body connection, we can start to see our lives in new and profound ways, making way for more space and less noise from the digital world. From here, we can begin to weave news, art, reading, podcasts, and media back into our daily lives without letting it knock us off our center. Each practice that we've integrated thus far has led us to better awareness of what takes our attention from us and what restores it. Now, it is time to take this another step further and finally dive into our creative practice—no matter if creativity is your job, hobby, side hustle, or literally a part of your DNA.

I have so many creative practices that are dear to my heart, but for the purpose of this chapter, I will discuss the two I find to be the most profound for me: dancing and quilting. These creative practices are tied to my job but are not currently my main sources of income. I am a dancer by training and degree and a quilter by study, but I do not make the majority of my income from selling these ephemeral or physical works. I do, however, make money teaching both, so there is a bit of crossover here with my research practice (more on this in the next chapter).

BENEFITS OF A CREATIVE PRACTICE

Consistent creative practice has the power to sharpen our mental faculties and offers us an amazing way to give back and be of service. We'll discuss this more in depth in chapter 10, but just know that anything you make or do creatively can be transformed and used to give back. Whether it's for a raffle, a gift, or fundraising effort, your creative practice can be a framework for giving to others.

Creative practice is also a way to clear the mental clutter, even if you face artistic blocks. While I love being detached from the outcome of my pursuits, I also love to tap into the magic of finishing a task. I know how satisfying it is to finish a quilt, and it's even more satisfying when that quilt raises thousands of dollars for a mutual aid fundraiser or is a beautiful wedding gift to a friend. If you find yourself often starting projects and not finishing them, picturing the finished product or making a list of what you could do with it are great ways to get to the finish line. At the same time, your practice doesn't have to be all about finishing. Like movement, what's most important here is the process and uncovering how creativity can shake out the mental debris of your day. It is yet another way to tap into the needs of your own spirit and redirect your attention to what nourishes you the most.

In chapter 5, I made sure to emphasize the importance of cultivating hobbies outside of your for-profit work. I encourage you to do the same with your creative practice, though it's not as necessary. An example of creativity and work crossing over in a positive way is if you are a ceramicist. For your job, you may have an online shop where you make functional objects like mugs, plates, and incense holders. This translates well for your creative practice because you won't need to build a whole new skill set. You might be able to work in the same medium but experiment with making different things in your free time. Maybe you want to make a series of lamps, try your hand at sculptural work, or collaborate with a local jewelry designer to create necklace beads.

There are so many ways you can expand your work to ensure you are still stoking your creative fire and passion. Figuring out what your personal creative practices are is an ongoing and ever-evolving journey, so be gentle with yourself as you try new things. You don't have to be good at anything creative; what's most important is that you're consistent. This does not mean you must do your creative work at the same time every day. In fact, I mean quite the opposite. My work and creative activities are incredibly seasonal, and I don't do them all the time. I will often plan and cut out many quilt projects at once, then slowly put them together over time. Or sometimes quilting activates my spinal pain so I can't work as often as I want. Likewise, there are seasons when I dance a lot, and there are other times dancing feels hard for me to access. In part, this is why I have many creative practices, so I can choose the ones that feel best to me through various cycles of life.

This is the real meaning of consistency: finding the rhythm and tempo that works for you and committing yourself to that ebb and flow.

THE RELATIONSHIP BETWEEN CREATIVITY AND ATTENTION

Creative acts and practices can bring us into a state of flow in a way that is different than many hobbies or work, allowing our ideas to emerge and our worries to slip away. We can find true presence in the creative portal of our lives, which allows us to sharpen our attention and improve our ability to be open and responsive rather than closed and reactive.

Again, consuming media, food, sex, screens, or whatever else you enjoy isn't inherently bad, but it's important that you stay aware of what it feels like when you move the needle too far and use them to fill the void of discomfort, avoidance, or lack of control. Creative activities that get you into flow states can work to rewire your brain and bring you into states that the body remembers before you began over-indulging. By committing to this practice, you will eventually find that you won't have to consciously choose a creative act every time you want to reach for something else. Instead, you will naturally start reaching for these habits less because your brain now desires creation over consumption. Similar to hobbies and movement, it is important to build in easy access to your creative process so you have the space to let yourself dream big and expand.

Pushing the limits of creativity can help bring you community, connection, and care. Here are a few ways you can go further in your creative practice than you probably are right now:

- Investing in a new sewing machine
- Building an art studio in your backyard
- Starting a shared sketchbook or mail-based project with a collaborator
- Using your local library for meetups
- Committing to ten minutes of uninterrupted creative time a day
- Writing a manifesto of your current art practice
- Renting an art studio outside the house
- Taking a class to learn more about your art practice
- Hosting a monthly art night in your living room
- Starting your own art collective

- Offering a free workshop to your community from your front porch
- Opening a gallery
- Starting an artist residency in a spare bedroom

While your movement practice works to calm your nervous system, your creative practice is here to help you re-center the mind and clear out the mental clutter that digital intake can create. But it's important to note that your creative work could land you back into the digital sphere if you're doing something like making memes or coding. In these cases, you will need to set even better boundaries around putting your phone down or closing your computer when you are done. This is why it's so important that you stay willing to pivot without judgment. Try your best not to judge your needs or actions or make up stories about them. With these new habits, you are working to challenge yourself without pushing your nervous system to a place that is unbearable and leads you to quit altogether.

FINDING YOUR CREATIVE PRACTICE

In order to find a practice that feels sustainable, even if it is seasonal, you'll want to reflect on what speaks to your interests. And similar to cultivating your hobbies, you have to be willing to be bad at some of them at first—or forever, to be honest. I have been quilting for twelve years, and I still make plenty of mistakes or get halfway through a project and absolutely hate it.

Art-making is a constant battle of figuring out what works and what doesn't, what pleases the muse and what is a disappointment, what brings you pleasure and what simply stresses you out.

One out-of-the-box project I've recently homed in on is changing the aesthetics of my house. I like it because it's totally separate from my job and isn't quite a hobby and isn't quite art, but picking paint swatches for the kitchen, doors, and outside trim stokes the creative flame within. Changing up something in your house with a can of paint is a great and relatively inexpensive way to change up the vibe and match your current mood. My bright yellow kitchen is one of my favorite parts of my house, and people are always amazed at how magnificent it is when they walk in.

Creating a beautiful home for yourself is a great way to flex your creative muscle, and it's a perfect way to double-dip with tasks. I will often listen to the news, a podcast, or an audiobook while I am painting or doing housework. This allows me to tap into the real world and my creative spirit at the same time. You could also put on a fun playlist and dance around as you work. The possibilities are limitless.

Working across mediums also gives you plenty to reach for when you're in different moods and tides of life. For example, quilting might be more meditative for you, while painting may feel more like a chore. This, of course, is totally dependent on your relationship to the mediums. Give yourself permission to switch it up and keep track of what creative acts work and feel best on certain days, in certain moods, or for certain needs.

My own practice of quilting has changed many times over the years. I was originally taught by one of my favorite artists, Eliza Fernand, who is a true researcher and devotee of the art of quilting. They have done so many projects around quilts, collecting stories of quilters around the country, creating shows and installations, teaching, painting quilt murals, and hosting residencies.

After Eliza taught me to quilt, I felt like for the first time I had a usable object I could translate my improvisational dance practice into. At the time, I was struggling with the ephemeral, nontangible nature of dance. Finishing my first quilt gave me the most satisfying feelings of completion that I will never forget, and that quilt is still very dear to me today. I made it with the thrifted tablecloths and napkins from my wedding to my former husband and quilted it to an old wool blanket my dad had used as a curtain in college. It worked as its own spell, and three years after we got divorced and John and I moved back in together to run an artist residency, it went back on the couch. Another spell. June eventually chewed some holes in it, but as an object it still remains solid.

In 2020, when everyone was in lockdown and sewing masks, I wondered if I could turn my in-person quilting class into an online offering. For many years "A Quilt is Something Human" was wildly successful, and alongside artist Christi Johnson, we taught hundreds of people how to quilt. Teaching, like quilting, is also a creative practice for me. While it falls more into my research practice, it is absolutely a place where I become creative and willing to expand as an artist. The more I teach quilting, the more I learn about it.

Quilting also gives me an entry point into anti-perfectionism, which I also believe to be a facet of unlearning white supremacy. In order to disrupt racism and systems of oppression, we must be willing to get messy, make mistakes, and jump in the pond of change. When I make a big mistake in my quilting or my lines aren't straight, I get to remember that this is not a reflection of my value as a person. Instead, I build on my capacity to fail and begin again. Going against what we've inherited or learned about ourselves and other people requires dedication and the willingness to be wrong.

Quilting as an art form provides me the pathway to get it wrong, to begin again, and to make it right. It lets me fold in mistakes and sew them down with a zig-zag stitch. It lets me find out about my own ancestors and guide others to learn about theirs. Quilting is an excellent entry point to learn about place, people, and process.

While having a final product is a beautiful part of creating, the process is just as important. Every time I make something, I learn lessons around how to be more gentle with myself and to accept both what has come and what is coming next.

Take a moment now to think of one or two creative practices you'd like to indulge in and fold them into your next attention audit or digital detox. Pick ones that are easy and effortless for you, not a heavy lift. Here are a few options to spark your creativity:

- Writing
- Painting
- Drawing
- Crafting
- Playing music
- Photography
- Coding
- Gardening
- Landscaping
- Making clothes
- Quilting
- Dancing
- Singing
- Writing poetry
- Playwriting
- Improv acting
- Comedy

One rule I follow to make things easy for me to engage with my creative practice is to set myself up for success. For example, whenever I am done with a sewing session, I always make sure my sewing machine is threaded and the bobbin is wound. This way, the next time I have a desire to sew, I can just sit down and start. Even though to a neurotypical person these might be very simple tasks to do before starting a creative project, they can be really hard for me and other neurodivergent folks. So part of ending my creative ritual is getting the space ready for the next time I have the impulse to do it.

NURTURING CREATIVE PRACTICE AS A DAILY HABIT

While I recognize that daily habits are not for everyone, I find that they've really helped me get into a groove and routine, especially with my creative practice. If you already know that daily habits do not work for you, feel free to skip this section. However, if there is a sliver of you that is curious about what I might have to say about them, keep reading.

The first important point I want to make about daily habits is that they don't have to be forever. You can try a daily habit for a container of time (a week is usually a good place to start) and see if it works for you. And depending on the activity you're trying to cultivate, it may be unrealistic to do it every day. For example, I certainly do not quilt every day, and while I do write almost every day, I certainly do not write every day in every season of life. Sometimes I am way more focused on quilting or dancing than I am with my writing. I do find though that consistency with my creative habits, even if I am switching them out, provides me with a better sense of flow.

While I was working on this book, I made it incredibly easy for myself to begin by clearly outlining what each step of the process would be. I woke up every morning at 5:00 am for months to finish it. Sometimes I would do this with others in my writing group, Landscapes, but for the final few weeks, I decided I needed to do it alone, to be in the duet of just me and the book. Writing every day at the same time with the same habits brought me a creative flow like I have never seen before. Over time, my body and mind knew how to sit down and write morning after morning. I would turn the coffee on, take my meds, go to the bathroom, feed June, let her out, light my candle, take a beautiful flower essence my friend Liz Migliorelli of Sister Spinster made me, let June in, fill my coffee cup, take a seat, turn on my twenty-five-minute timer, and write.

Consider trying something every day for a week, or even every week for a month, to build the habit of a consistent practice. It could be a movement you enjoy, a new hobby you've picked up, or even a creative practice you've just decided on. I'll admit, it'll likely be challenging to stick to at first, but you'll be surprised how quickly it becomes second nature.

If you're concerned about your ability to stick to your commitment, perhaps you can try enlisting some public accountability either online or among family and friends. From September 2015 to late 2016, I completed a project called "Personal Practice," where every day I made a dance video and posted it to a social media account. I never missed a day. In some ways, it started by accident. In July of 2015, I started posting dance videos when I felt like it, but by October, I realized I had made one every day for a month and decided to try to do it for a full year. I carried on the project off and on for a decade. Although I began the challenge on my own, I believe the public accountability was what kept me going for so long. Saying you are going to do something, even to just one person, opens up a portal of accountability that can lead you to a consistent creative practice.

At the end of the day, your creativity is 100 percent personal. Whether it's wearing new outfits, hosting a clothing or book swap with friends, getting a cool haircut, wearing fun makeup, or getting Gel-X nails, let your creativity fuel everything you do. Suddenly, you will find that you have a very creative life and a strong handle on where your attention goes. When creativity is a non-negotiable part of your day, you will be met with a new level of discipline and devotion. Not discipline in an authoritative kind of a way, but in the sense that you are clear on what you are devoted to and its purpose.

Now that you've taken some time to think about your potential creative pursuits, make a list of why you are devoted to your creative practice or, if you are just starting out, what a creative practice might bring to your life. There may be times you need a break from your creative pursuits, and that's okay, but your devotion will be your guide to let you know when you are taking a break because you truly need one and when you are in a state of avoidance.

OVERCOMING CREATIVE BLOCKS AND SELF-DOUBT

Creative blocks happen to all of us. But overcoming a creative block isn't about finding ways to never have them anymore; it is about finding ways to approach them that allow us to carry on with our work anyway. When I hit a creative block, I always go back to a concept I learned a few years ago in therapy called the

Emotional Car. When big emotions come in, like fear of failure, self-judgment, or anxiety, we do not put them in the trunk of the car, close the door, and hope they never re-emerge. We also do not let them drive the car. Instead, we sit in the driver's seat and put fear, judgment, and anxiety in the back seat. We invite them along for the ride. They are not allowed to touch the radio dial or change the channel, but they are allowed to listen and respond to our questions.

We can ask fear, "Why are you here? What are you trying to protect me from?" Often, the negative feelings that come up around creative practice have to do with our fears of failure or embarrassment, and we assume that if we never try at all, we won't fail at the thing we are attempting to do. Guess what? This is true! But there's a caveat. Without risk, sure, there is no failing, but there is also no growth. There is only stasis. And that is not what we are here for. We are here to expand and serve, create and delight, and to mix it all together for magic and mystery.

External distractions can also be a huge block to our creativity. Work, family, the phone, and home responsibilities can pull us away from our creative acts. See to it that you protect your time in every realm of practice, whether you tell your family to leave you be for thirty minutes so you can create, or you change your phone setting to do not disturb, airplane mode, or my favorite phone position yet: OFF. All of this can help tune out any outside noise that prevents you from entering a flow state.

Another tool I use when I am feeling blocked in any medium, including writing, is to freewrite in my journal for fifteen minutes. With this practice, I don't attempt to be creative or profound; I just dump words on the page to clear my head, no matter how nonsensical my sentences are. This always provides me with a nice break from thinking about my work too much and instead forces me to think more about the internal landscape of my experience and my reaction to it.

You can also lean heavily on your movement practice to get through blocks. If you've been painting for a few hours, taking a break to walk around the block is a great restart. Sometimes the breaks come naturally to us, and sometimes we really need to structure them and put them on a timer. Doing jumping jacks, getting a small trampoline or jump rope, or stretching on a mat are all movement breaks you can take to get back into a creative flow. And who knows—these breaks might be just what you need to flood you with more ideas. It's so easy for us to think pushing through is how we are going to get things done, but resting and giving the mind and body a break are sometimes the best ways to allow ideas to flow.

Creative blocks are a part of the process, so it's important that we greet them with kindness, invite them into the backseat, and drive on into the sunset of art, design, and creation. Our creative blocks often arise when our attention is fragmented, and it is my experience that the more I heal my attention, the more I am able to focus on creative projects for long periods of time. These tools go hand in hand. The more you focus on creativity, the more your attention will heal. And the more you restore your focus, the more your creative practice will flourish.

I also encourage you to find ways to be playful during creative blocks. Put on fun music, use new colors, and try not to take your practice so seriously. When we hold our creative practice with a looser grip, we can more easily find play and fun in the process. This then translates to other areas of our life. When big mistakes happen or even small misunderstandings, we no longer blow them out of proportion; we can see them as right-sized and move forward.

REFLECT

What helps you soften when you hit a creative block? Make a short list of methods, rituals, and tools that you'd like to lean on when resistance shows up. Here are a few of my ideas:

- Make something intentionally bad or cheesy—don't filter yourself

- Set a timer for five minutes of minimal effort

- Move your body—even a quick walk around the block can help

- Work in a different medium (I like collaging or mood-boarding on my tablet)

- Talk it out with a creative friend

- Take a purposeful break with no guilt

THE HEALING POWER OF CREATIVE PRACTICE

Creative practice to me is the root of all healing. It is the beginning of being of service, of being able to offer something back to others that inspires and ripples outward, creating an effect that brings more people closer to their own desire for creation and art. Our creative pursuits are not simply intellectual or artsy exercises; they are deeply healing acts that bring the mind, body, and spirit back into alignment when our attention is fractured beyond measure.

Creativity is an act of self-care, especially if you feel a call toward it. Denying yourself your creative practice is denying an intrinsic part of who you are and what you need to process the world. Having this outlet, whether it is tied to your profession or not, gives you a place to work through unresolved emotions and release stress and fear. It is an outlet for expression, even if you never show it to anyone, that brings you into greater alignment with the self.

While I am a true believer in the power of sharing our art, this is not a requirement for creative practice. You could color in a coloring book every day and never show anyone. This is still your creative practice that will serve you. I do, however, encourage you to share your original creations. To me, this is the key difference between hobbies and art-making. Hobbies can be private, but creative practice is for the people. Art is for an audience.

Don't start there, though, thinking about who it is for (unless, of course, this is helpful for you). Your creative process is about your agenda and your expectations, not anyone else's. It's easy to think of all the ways someone might not like your creative work, and it's true; people might hate it! But don't let that stop you from expressing yourself. For example, I find a strange pleasure in reading some of my worst book reviews on Goodreads, but I don't let that stop me from writing other books.

Creative practice is an ongoing journey that requires us to explore, make mistakes, and change our daily routines and habits for the better. It is a central part of healing our attention span and learning to tend to ourselves rather than everything or everyone around us. We start with the simple fact that we need to create in order to survive. The audience and the platform to share it on will come later through our research and service.

Stay committed to developing your creative practice in a way that feels right and joyful to you. If it starts to feel like a chore or a drain, change it up. Make the time, even if it is brief. There are so many ways to be an artist, a creator, and a devotee to the creative process. May your creative practice be rooted in openness and curiosity. May it shine through everything you do. May you be the driver of your own creative destiny.

8

RESEARCH PRACTICE

We live in capitalism, its power seems
inescapable—but then so did the divine
right of kings. Any human power can be
resisted and changed by human beings.
Resistance and change often begin in art.
Very often in our art, the art of words.

—Ursula K. Le Guin, Speech in Acceptance of the National
Book Foundation Medal for Distinguished Contribution
to American Letters

Research is not solely an academic practice; it is a practice that everyone can integrate into their lives whether they're part of an institution or not. Research involves anything you want to look into further through reading, writing, study, or teaching that brings you pleasure and satisfaction. It could be as simple as learning the history of your favorite flower, mapping the migratory path of birds in your region, or collecting family or neighborhood recipes and making a little zine. Or it could be as complex as studying queer mysticism, Indigenous histories, and contemporary dynamics of your small town; analyzing urban design patterns; or interviewing local artists for an oral history project. Embracing the art of research filled my life with new purpose and meaning and continues to give me new ideas for my creative work. Much of my research around quilts, dance, and history has been completely self-led or in collaboration with friends who were interested in the same topics.

Research challenges our perspectives of the world, giving us new insights and materials to work with in our hobbies, creative practices, and work. Research allows us to tap into flow and find more presence in the rabbit holes we find ourselves too enthralled in to pull ourselves out. Research is mind-expanding, giving us the freedom to seek understanding in everything that interests us.

Although many of us are most familiar with intentional academic research, we can also undergo natural research over our lifetime. As an example, I am always in the process of researching quilts. Whether it's reading about them, watching documentaries, teaching and taking classes, collecting books, or studying patterns, I am always immersed in the research of quilts. Finding a topic for steady and consistent research is special because it gives you an entry point into studying everything else. From studying how quilts came to be in the States, I was able to understand the racial divide in the formation of the United States in a clearer way, track how different patterns emerged from colonized regions, and see what lineages have been erased or carried on. The research of something as simple as quilts has inadvertently brought me closer to understanding people and place, giving me a starting point to build new relationships in community. It also has given me an entry point to become closer to neighbors in my region across class, race, and generations—just by asking, "Do you quilt?"

Research also helps us remain focused by bringing our attention to something that matters to us. Replacing digital habits and reclaiming our attention can take great effort and mental agility, so finding things that light us up and make us want to learn more gives us greater insight and expands our imagination. When I was in the throes of my social media and email addiction, I would sometimes feel like I didn't care about anything, like everything was boring and not worth my attention. After all, why would I dive into deep research when I could read a short infographic instead?

Healing our attention must always come from two directions: putting down the digital distractions and filling that void with our practices. It is a dance between the two that requires daily examination of when to pick something up, when to put it down, and what to replace our reaching with (more on this in the next chapter). Our creative horizons are asking us to lean into learning so we can better understand ourselves and the world and pass our knowledge to others.

READING AS CREATIVE RESEARCH

It is not my job to be a journalist or a reporter, but it is my job to do my research and be an active participant of the world. Like many people, specifically white people, I spent a good portion of my undergraduate years, the big year of 2020, and beyond deepening my unlearning of white supremacy and internalized racism. In 2023, I became more aware of the history of Palestine and Israel. Of course, this work of learning and unlearning is never done, but there are many times in the process when I felt overwhelmed and late to the table. In those instances, I turned to documentaries and books that touched on specific topics of interest.

In my effort to learn as much as I could about the history of the Palestinian people and their land, I gravitated to books like *Palestinian Walks* by Raja Shehadeh and *Recognizing the Stranger: On Palestine and Narrative* by Isabella Hammad. I wanted to learn the history of the people and place through two of my own practices: walking and writing.

In my dedication to unlearning white supremacy, a book that really spoke to me was Resmaa Menakem's *My Grandmother's Hands* because it led from a somatic place, unpacking how racism lives in the body and ways we can begin to move through that. I could name so many books that have helped in my research, but I mention all of this to say that your research doesn't have to be tied to any particular outcome, container, or project. While I do think those can be helpful, there are simply some themes and topics that require our dedicated learning over the course of a lifetime. Find something that speaks to your interests, so that the unlearning is just as important as the learning. So that the unwinding is just as thrilling as what lights you up.

The power of reading in creative research is an extremely important part of reclaiming our attention and focus. More than any other task, reading is what I lost the most during my digital addiction and what I hear from others is the hardest to regain. Creating a disciplined reading practice, finding something you are excited to read about, and detoxing from the digital realm are all integral parts of reclaiming this skill.

I acknowledge that this is easier said than done. Reclaiming reading as a practice is probably the hardest and most frustrating part of regaining control of your attention span. But I also know you can do it because I was able to. My attention was truly so fractured that I could barely open a book, let alone read a full page. The idea of failing at reading after not doing it for so long was so overpowering that I couldn't even think about picking up a book.

To regain my reading skills and confidence in myself, I had to completely give up social media. There was no middle ground for me. As long as I continued to produce and read short captions, watch fifteen-second reels, and fill my brain with fast facts, the less I was able to strengthen my capacity to take in long-form information. I am not saying you need to quit social media in order to read a book, but if you find that you struggle to consume long-form content, this may be a helpful step to take.

In Carl Phillips' book *My Trade is Mystery* he writes, "As long as I am living in language, as I like to put it, I count it as writing. This is why reading—for example—is so important—is maybe the most important part of writing. If I'm reading, I'm also at some level taking in language's capacities and variations for the expression of human experience." I feel it is this—this living in the human experience—that is why we must read and write. To be in the throes of the living.

Once I understood what was holding me back from cultivating a reading practice, I had to do the work of setting myself up for success. I began by committing to a nightly reading session. I made sure to leave my phone in another room, power down my computer, and create a calming, distraction-free space. This way, when I got in bed, I had whatever book I was reading, my to-do list notebook, and my morning pages notebook. For one to two hours before I fell asleep, I would journal, jot down things I wanted to do the next day, and read my book. It was difficult at first to keep my attention on these tasks, but over time, with dedicated practice, they slowly but surely became my way of winding down from the day.

Reading fosters deep attention, stokes our imagination and creativity, and is one of the fastest ways to train yourself to be able to pay attention to anything for more than two minutes at a time. Cultivating a reading practice may require you to set some strict boundaries for yourself at first, similar to what I did with my nightly routine. You could set a goal to read ten pages before bed each night, read one chapter of a novel every day after work, or even finish one book a week.

I find that word count goals really help me when I am writing, but for reading I like to keep it to specific times and let myself go as long or short as I want. I try not to put too much pressure on it.

You don't have to become an avid reader overnight. You can try turning the volume up by just 1 percent each day or week. Something to help you simply dip in and start the practice. Regardless of what goal you set for yourself, protecting your reading time from outside distractions is of utmost importance, otherwise you'll constantly be tempted to check your notifications or texts, which makes it much harder to get into a flow. Getting back into reading can take a lot of practice, and I really do mean that. You will likely fail, make mistakes, and have to experiment, start over, and try again. I know I did. But eventually, you will find what works for you, and, as always, this is subject to change. I restarted my reading practice with a nightly session in bed, but sometimes I like to read on the couch by the fire or take a book to a local coffee shop and relax. Find what allows you to get lost in reading and trust that.

Another aspect of a reading practice that could increase your chances of success is having a wide range of things to read and formats to indulge in. Although I am a nonfiction lover, I keep a diverse rotation of books on my nightstand to keep my mind engaged. Whether it's a book for school, something about the world or history, a self-help book, a craft book, or even the rare fiction or poetry book, I need to have different books available for different times of day, different moods, and different desires. I am ever-changing, so naturally my reading choices will also shift. I also noticed I like to listen to finance audiobooks, but I prefer to read history or current events. For my research, I like to print out PDFs so I'm able to mark up the pages with pen, highlighter, and sticky note flags.

It is also important that you step out of your comfort zone every now and then and read books outside of your interests. For years, I only read books about self-improvement, but there was only so much improving I could do before it was time to learn about other things that were happening or have happened in the world. I found that branching out and exploring other subjects, ideas, and genres changed the way I saw the world and helped to deeply heal my attention.

Giving myself permission to read during the day and releasing the guilt I felt for doing so was another big breakthrough for me in releasing myself from productivity and work addiction, as well as figuring out how to get my attention back. There is something so luxurious about sitting down and reading for pleasure, school, research, or work during the afternoon hours, and in some ways, I feel like I shouldn't be allowed to do such a thing. This is usually a time when most people are deep in their work or email inbox, and they feel like they don't have space to devote ten minutes of their time to some leisure reading or casual research. I completely understand this, and perhaps nights and weekends really do work best for you and your schedule. But if you have a spare ten minutes or so to transport your mind to another place or time, I encourage you to do so—and don't feel bad about it!

Regardless of what you choose to read and research, allow your reading practice to be creative fuel that brings you closer to other forms of research, like writing, teaching, or sharing your insights. Reading is not just about absorbing information; it is a practice of attunement. It allows us to stretch our attention, expand our worldview, and nourish our inner life. This is the foundation of how you can grow as a human and invest in your relationship with your attention.

REFLECT

- What kind of reader are you right now? What kind of reader do you want to be?

- Are there genres, authors, or topics you've been curious about but haven't explored yet?

- When and where do you feel the most able to read with presence? The morning, after work, before bed?

- What gets in the way of reading consistently, and how might you gently shift that?

- What small reading goal can you set for yourself this month? Perhaps you could even do it alongside a friend to keep each other accountable.

Let this be a moment of realignment, not judgment, with your reading practice and creative life. This is not a task or a chore, but a gift of pleasure.

WRITING AS CREATIVE RESEARCH

You do not have to be a writer to find purpose and passion in the written word. Writing is a mode of research, communication, and contemplative study that comes in many different forms, from morning pages, creative journals, and to-do lists to newsletters, zines, essays, and more. Each container has its own purpose and reasoning behind it, and it's likely that you already regularly engage in some form of writing practice. For instance, my morning pages journal is for any brain-dumping flow that I want to get out. It is not necessarily for creative writing, although big ideas can spark from it, which is why I usually have my to-do list journal close by to jot down anything I want to look up later. I find this contemplative practice to be incredibly important for regulating my nervous system, reclaiming my attention, and igniting new ideas for creative practice.

Having a container for your writing will give shape to your other forms of research. I am such a big fan of self-publishing and have self-published three books and multiple zines. Although I write all the time, going down the self-publishing path offered me the freedom to explore and share any topic I wanted to without the input of a company, organization, or publisher. There are so many ways to be creative with your writing and how you share it. Even if you're not interested in publishing your writing, you can share any notes, insights, or ideas you have with others via email newsletters, blog posts, or even typed notes on your phone. The containers for writing are truly infinite, so I encourage you to pick one and see where it takes you.

Similar to reading, setting aside specific times for your writing practice is essential to be consistent. You could choose to write for ten to fifteen minutes every day, use the pomodoro method to incorporate some small dopamine breaks, or join a writing group that meets at certain times each week or month. Whatever you decide to do, it is important that you find the right amount of time and right time of day that best serves your energy levels, attention span, and ability to focus. It could be helpful to revisit your attention audit so you can understand your many natural cycles, which may coincide with the cycles of the seasons, your menstrual cycle, or lunar cycles.

In addition to the cognitive benefits, writing can also help you track your progress across disciplines. The more you write, the more you will be able to see the quality of your writing improve, and this is true for specific forms of writing as well. For example, the more you practice making gratitude lists, the more you'll be able to see how your gratitude shifts through various stages of life. And the more you journal, the more you'll see the patterns in your moods, thought processes, and life events. Writing is a tracking practice, one that allows you to become intimate with your internal and external forms, and combined with research, it gives you a place to understand the world and your own habits in a new way.

Even if you don't consider yourself to be a writer, I encourage you to develop a writing habit, both in service to your research and to yourself. Start small with just one journal page or five minutes of freewriting in your spare time. See if there is something you already do during the day that could coincide with a contemplative writing practice, or perhaps give yourself time in the morning before everyone wakes up. As an example, I prefer to do my creative writing in the predawn hours because everything feels so quiet, my brain is sharp, and I haven't started my work with others yet.

Find your writing container, find your time slots, and keep experimenting with them. See how writing can stretch your attention to new places. Try your hand at writing a poem, a research paper, or a newsletter—the opportunities are endless! Writing is not about perfection, but the constant evolution of new ideas and how they can serve the people, both publicly and privately.

REFLECT

- What kind of writing feels most natural and exciting to you right now?

- When, during your day or week, do you feel most clear-headed and open to writing?

- What blocks or patterns have kept you from writing consistently in the past?

- What kind of environment helps you write? Quiet coffee shop, alone at home, in community with others, by natural light, by candlelight?

- How do you want your writing to support your life emotionally, intellectually, spiritually, or professionally?

Take the time to plant a seed for a routine that supports—not pressures—your writing life.

TEACHING AS CREATIVE RESEARCH

You may not consider yourself a teacher or be interested in the art of teaching, but I believe anyone who is actively learning something new can also become a teacher of that thing, even as a humble beginner. Teaching our creative practices, whether formally or informally, is one of the most powerful ways to research and refine our work. Whether you are teaching a university course, hosting a book club in your living room, or simply sharing the information you've learned with a friend, teaching is one of the most powerful ways we can dedicate ourselves to creative research and the practice of attention.

For me, teaching helps me clarify my ideas and go even deeper into the history and roots of whatever I am teaching. I have primarily taught quilting over the last few years, and I am always in a state of wonder with how much more I've had to learn in order to teach properly. The most important thing is I didn't wait to become an expert to teach a class on quilt-making. I became a total fanatic, integrated the teaching skills I had learned in the past from witnessing my own teachers across many disciplines, and then I started myself. You don't need a perfect rule book to become a teacher. In fact, people gravitated toward my quilt class *because* I wasn't an expert, because my lines were wonky, and because I took a nontraditional approach to the practice. It was my imperfections that made me the perfect teacher for certain students.

I once got anonymous feedback from a student that said, "I could have learned all of this on YouTube." At the time I remember that really hurting me until I realized, *Why yes, dear student, you can learn how to do almost anything on YouTube or at your local library.* But what we can't get from YouTube is the community aspect of sharing and reporting back in a classroom setting. This is irreplaceable, and this is what makes being in the classroom setting, for both the student and the teacher, so transformative.

By clarifying our ideas, teaching gives us space to deepen our understanding of our practice. When I prepare to teach a class, I often work both backward and forward. For instance, I might discover something new that I am really interested in and then want to teach a class about it. This is where my research guides my teaching. Or I might think of a class I want to teach, then dive into deep research to support my knowledge base. This is where my teaching influences my research practice. They live harmoniously together as one big process, diverting my attention away from screens to the beauty of learning and self-growth.

I also find that, by teaching others, my own skills and craft are refined and expanded. When I find different ways to explore or present a topic, I learn new things about the work itself. Even more profoundly, my students most often end up pouring back into me with their inquisitive questions and desire to deepen their own studies. In quilt class, we all take the month to study our personal ancestry and textile lineage, then report it back to each other in a show-and-tell format. These sessions are emotional, enlivening, and completely transformative, and I always end up learning something I never knew before.

Speaking of emotions, it's okay to be emotional when you teach! We should always be questioning what professionalism is, what it looks like, and how we can be our full selves in front of our students and peers. The morning after the Club Q shooting in 2022, I saddled up to teach a quilt class. I often begin this class by reading an excerpt from the chapter "We Bring a Quilt," about the AIDS Memorial Quilt, from Cleve Jones' autobiography, *When We Rise: My Life in the Movement*. Reading it out loud is a pleasure, as it is an incredibly powerful piece, but being a queer person, reading to a Zoom room full of queer and trans people after witnessing yet another mass shooting, I began to weep. And then I began to sob uncontrollably. In the moment, I felt so incredibly embarrassed and unprofessional, like I was letting my students down. But when I finally looked up, many were crying with me and had left affirming notes in the chat. It was a big moment in my career where I realized the line between student and teacher doesn't have to be so stark. In fact, we can blend as a non-hierarchical group who are learning and exploring together.

When I am done teaching, I often like to cool down a bit with some journaling. It can be easy for me to pick apart every little thing I did and feel like it wasn't good enough. So in an effort to offer myself grace in a space of self-critique, I like to jot down a couple notes of what went well, what I might do differently next time, and how I want to proceed with my research. I also like to consult with a friend to let them know I am about to teach. That way, I can share any stage fright beforehand, check in with them about how it went, and talk through any ruminating self-doubt afterward.

I have also been experimenting with what I call the "Zoom room arrival practice." Some might call it a grounding exercise but that felt too cheesy to me, so I had to name it something else. It is different every time and I make it up as I go, but it lets me and my students arrive as we are, get more comfortable, and coregulate in the digital space before we dive in together.

In Landscapes, my co-working group, I also make up an opening theme song for each Zoom session. This is also my way of making the space fun and pleasurable to me and everyone who arrives—finding ways to make research and teaching fun is at the core of my practice.

So far, I've talked mostly about traditional teaching in a class-like setting, but there are so many ways and styles of teaching, so get creative! Your particular teaching muscle could be flexed in nontraditional ways, like teaching your kid to ride a bike, volunteering to teach incarcerated people how to write or make a craft, working with youth at your local community center, or teaching a friend how to make your favorite dish. Teaching doesn't have to be exactly linked to your job. It can be linked to a hobby, a spiritual practice, or any other aspect of your personal life.

Regardless of how you decide to teach and what you choose to share with others, teaching is a way to reinforce and more deeply understand the knowledge you are researching. It invites you to step into a different kind of attention, one that requires clarity, empathy, and creative translation. This, in turn, will help bring your attention into a sharp, clear focus and move the needle of your awareness forward.

REFLECT

- What have you learned, lived, or explored that you feel excited to share with others?

- Who do you imagine benefitting most from what you know (e.g., friends, artists, students, community members)?

- What teaching style feels most aligned with your energy (e.g., one-on-one mentorship, casual group discussions, online co-working groups, recorded videos, hands-on workshops, a PDF guide, etc.)?

- What settings feel right for your teaching style (e.g., teaching indoors or outdoors, in homes, in classrooms, in person, online)?

- What scares you about teaching? What excites you?

- How can you regulate your nervous system and lessen your anxiety to prepare to teach?

Let these questions be a place to start dreaming. Teaching doesn't have to be formal or traditional; it can be as simple as starting a conversation, writing a how-to guide, or sharing your notes in a newsletter.

CREATE A RESEARCH PLAN

Integrating research—whether through reading, writing, or teaching—into your creative routine is vital for continual growth, the expansion of your ideas, and the reclamation of your attention. It is essential to help you come back into focus with the world after months or maybe even years of being a distracted vessel with nowhere to put your curiosity. It's important that you know where to put your knowledge, even if it is just a spot on the wall where you can tape pieces of paper with lists upon lists.

One of my favorite ways to ensure I integrate my research instead of just collecting piles of data is by creating a research plan. I had the great pleasure of attending Goddard College for one semester before they closed, and creating my plan for the semester was one of the most luxurious and satisfying things I have ever done. I was able to create my own assignments, reading lists, and study goals in collaboration with my professor, for both the semester and the whole year. I often teach people how to map out the quarters of their year in business, and in many ways, I learned this from creating these documents. I would hole up in the library on the Vermont campus for hours, poring over books and researching every single thing I could come up with about quilts, Indigenous teaching and research methods, Swedish textile and quilt history, dance, and more. It was a beautiful way to see how all my interests came together in one study plan.

To create a research plan, it's best to start with your timelines, both big and small. When I am looking at a year, I typically work with three timelines: the year itself, the quarters, and the months; but you can choose whatever timelines make the most sense to you. Once you have your timelines down, make a list of everything you want to study. Any topics at all. They don't have to be related to each other. Let's say from April to June, you want to study gardening and prepare your garden for planting seeds and new plants as spring emerges. You'll want to make a list of texts you will read, field trips you'll go on, and anyone you might want to connect with or interview about gardening to expand your knowledge.

Do this for each subject you want to learn more about. An interest in horseback riding might bring you to volunteer at a local stable, read a novel about horses, or watch the heartbreaking film *Wild Hearts Can't Be Broken*. Let your research plan be thoughtful and a reflection of your true desires. Once you've done this, you can print it out, put it in a cute binder, or hang it on your wall as a constant reminder.

This research plan is also a great way to track your progress and growth. Make it a point to check back in on your sheet and see which activities you've done, what books you've read, which people you've reached out to, and feel free to set more goals or milestones if you feel you need them. The point of this exercise is to make research a foundational place to redirect your attention, so be sure you're focusing your time and energy on the interests that light you up.

CREATING RITUAL AROUND YOUR RESEARCH

In the next chapter, we'll speak more deeply about creating rituals throughout the day that support all of your many projects, responsibilities, and work, but for now, let's discuss how you can ritualize your research practice.

As you'll soon learn, ritual is an important part of what it means to be human, and whether you realize it or not, you engage in some form of ritual each day. It's what gets you into a groove in the morning and what helps you settle your nervous system at night. When it comes to research, ritualizing the process can be just what you need to get you excited about your work and learning journey.

For me, my morning writing ritual begins with me lighting a candle and taking a flower essence to support me with my projects. My brain now knows that when the candle is lit, it is time to focus. The same can be said for my nighttime routine. When I've reached the end of my workday, I like to shut my computer down completely, put it in another room, and begin brewing some tea. I don't even think too hard about what tea I want or if I even really want tea; I just take the next action. Shut computer down, close computer, put computer away, fill tea kettle. From there, the next steps arrive naturally: I pick a tea and a mug, pour myself a hefty portion, and drink while I read. These simple rituals help me access my research in a way that feels like a soft landing place and gives my mind permission to relax and let the knowledge flow in.

I encourage you to create a ritual around your research practice, no matter what it looks like, whether it's five minutes of online exploration or a week-long trip to another country. You are invited to engage in this process however it best fits into your life. The point is not to add more work, stress, or to-dos, but to redefine how and what you like to learn both in and out of an academic setting. Research is a wonderful gateway to healing our attention, pulling us away from distractions, and fueling our creativity and passions.

OVERCOMING THE CHALLENGES OF A RESEARCH PRACTICE

Creative research can be overwhelming at times, but recognizing the barriers and developing strategies can help make it a more integrated and rewarding part of your practice. You might feel like you don't have enough time to dive as deep as you want to, and that is completely understandable. But I invite you to give yourself some grace and see if you can increase your practice by just 1 percent each time. What if you dedicate five minutes a day to reading about the history of where you live or writing a letter before you go to bed? Get creative here about how you can organize your time and your research in a way that expands your life, not shrinks it. Five minutes of your practice will always be better than not doing it at all.

A block I often face is not knowing where to begin. This is partly why I absolutely love libraries and archives. They give me the space and opportunity to grab as many books as I want and spread out for the day. Start with any topic you are interested in and see what jumps out at you. You could even listen to podcasts about the subject and follow the rabbit hole from there. There is absolutely no perfect place to start. You can start anywhere. Don't let the overwhelm get you down.

If you're anything like me, you love to archive your work and keep everything filed away for safe keeping. This is where Google Docs comes in handy. To me, there is nothing like the fresh energy of an empty Google Doc. I title the document according to the project I am working on or the thing I am researching, and I save it in a folder called PROJECTS so I can quickly reference it later.

Last year I completed a research project on the poet Joanne Kyger. I started with her book *Strange Big Moon*, a collection of her journals. While I had been a fan of her poetry for years, I hadn't locked into some of her other writing and teaching, and this project introduced me to new information about Joanne herself as well as journal-keeping as a practice. As the research project unfolded, I soon saw what it needed to become: a class on contemplative journaling practices taught through the lens of her work. The Google Doc I used throughout the project housed all of my writing, tabs, bibliography, and all the materials that could later become a sales page, a syllabus, and a document for the students to understand my process. Research involves a lot of trial and error, but you'll be surprised at what juicy revelations come about from simply diving in.

If you still find yourself getting stuck, bored, or distracted, this is often a sign that it's time to pivot to a new medium or a new topic. Take note of this. Boredom is often a sign that we are not getting enough of what we need. While I love the idea that we should make more time to be bored, in this context, it might be best to switch it up.

Sometimes if I have reached a stuck point, it actually means it's time for me to teach or share what I have learned so far or get private feedback from a friend. You don't necessarily need to wait to be done with a project before sharing it with others; their feedback might be just what you need to spark your curiosity again and the fuel you need to keep working. This is the magic of storytelling and connection, of trusting what happens when you are engaged with what lights you up.

RESEARCH AS A LIFELONG CREATIVE PRACTICE

Remember not to rush. Tending to our attention, our creativity, and our output as creative beings is a lifelong practice. And reading, writing, teaching, and studying are the foundational points of our research. These can be done in pleasure and with rigor. They can be done with ease in the company of others or in complete solitude. Regardless of what you choose, everything you are doing here—the attention audit, the digital detox, your practices—is all about curiosity over perfection. You will be clunky along the way, distractions will emerge, and your faith will be tested, but I'm confident that, as an ode to your fellow humans and planet, you will carry forth!

These are your practices to weave together to form the tapestry of your research work, however you may see it fitting into your life. Perhaps you want to make a podcast, complete an oral history project, or self-publish a catalog to go with an art show you're having. Research can take many forms, and there are many ways to organize it. I always love to think of dancer and choreographer Twyla Tharp's banker's boxes for each of her projects, where she puts all the ephemera, scraps of fabric, and tapes that inspire her process. You could do the same in Google Docs, notes on your phone, a binder, or folders.

I invite you to embrace research not as a static task, but as a dynamic practice. The process of research is not just about gathering information; it is about nurturing the seeds of your creativity and letting it bloom. The beauty of creative research is that it never ends; it continues to unfold with every new question, every new insight, and every new way of thinking. May your research delight you. May it be of service to the people and the planet. May it fill your cup so you are less distracted. May it be a gift to go down the rabbit hole.

9

SPIRITUAL PRACTICE

Before you scoff at the mention of spiritual practice or get scared I'll use the word "god" too much, just know that like every practice we've discussed so far, this is an experiment in figuring out what is right for you. Take what you like and leave the rest. In this chapter, I'll speak generally about my rituals, beliefs, and ideas that come from a combination of Buddhist study, pagan rituals, the Unitarian Universalist Church, Julia Cameron's *The Artist's Way*, over a decade in twelve-step programs, and the influence of many Jewish and Muslim friends who have shared their version of god and spirituality with me.

To put it simply, I believe in an all-knowing creator that is genderless and expansive, spacious and loving, forgiving and a part of everything. To me, god is the clouds and the lake and the blades of grass. Spirituality is a path we lay down ourselves that can include goddesses, ancestors, spirits, angels, or no entities at all. It can be the simple lighting of a candle to say thank you to whatever goodwill and good energy kept you alive another day, or it can look more traditional like a daily devotional or church service.

Regardless of what it means to you, a spiritual practice offers us a powerful antidote to the isolation and fragmentation that technology often fosters, helping us reconnect with ourselves, others, and the world around us and giving us something to hold on to when we feel like we don't know where or what to grasp. It is self-defined and can be practiced alone or in a group.

BENEFITS OF A SPIRITUAL PRACTICE

Years ago, a mentor of mine asked me what I was *really* looking for when I reached for my phone each day, and without skipping a beat, I said, "god." I was looking for the feeling of spiritual aliveness in my phone, but over the years, I have come to truly accept that god does not live in my phone. God lives in the everywhere and the everything and the nothingness. Although god may speak to me and share spiritual messages through the people in my phone, I am unlikely to find a deep spiritual solution to my problems on a social media feed.

Spirituality, and the practices that come with it, will look very personal to you. It could be praying on your knees, journaling, meditating, walking in nature, pulling tarot cards, or going to church, but I challenge you to experiment with something new and see if it works for you. Consider looking into your lineage and seeing what those who came before you traditionally practiced as rituals or ceremonies.

For me, my spiritual practice is rooted in being totally disconnected from all other practices. It supports each thing I do without being a part of it exactly. My spiritual practice is very private. I don't post pictures of it or share details very often, and I think keeping your spiritual practice offline and away from too many prying eyes will help center you and promote a deeper connection to Source/Higher Power/spirit of the universe/god/whatever you want to call it.

Finding a belief in something outside of ourselves—whether it's the belief that the sun will always rise and set or that a new moon will be full again—is a great benefit to our creative practices. When we are lost in doubt or uncertainty, faith reminds us that there are forces moving beyond our control, and that change is always underway. It gives us a framework of trust that our creative cycles will return when we stray, that rest is an important part of the process, and that we do not have to hold everything alone. These mystical tides and seasons are proven in science, but magical in their consistency.

Spiritual practice helps center our attention on a particular task or prayer, helping us heal our addiction to whatever is distracting us from what I have come to know as a "god-sized hole." This, in essence, is a void inside of us that developed from something we lacked as children, in a certain relationship, or by living under the system of capitalism. I say it's the size of god because only a spiritual remedy can fill it. No matter how hard we try, we cannot fill the god-sized hole with shopping, TV, social media, external validation, or any other habit. We must fill it with connection to spirit, to others, to the land, and to ourselves. Remember that god is both inside of you and outside of you. Giving yourself opportunities to deepen all of these connections through a spiritual practice will quiet your desire to constantly scroll or numb yourself with unhelpful methods.

Life in our modern world can be completely draining in so many ways, and devoting yourself to your spiritual practice is a way to fill your cup when all you want to do is numb out. I find that sitting down with a deck of tarot cards and my favorite tarot book, trancestor Rachel Pollack's *Seventy-Eight Degrees of Wisdom*, helps me find the ordinary magic I was looking for in my phone. I just often need the reminder that magic is everywhere, all around me.

Spirituality offers us a grounding presence when we feel so fractured from day-to-day life. In this grounded space, more closely tethered to your body, heart, and mind, you'll be able to approach all of your other practices with a sense of awe and wonder rather than obligation. For me, the chaos of digital life slips away as soon as I light a candle, take a flower essence, and read my daily prayer books. And like everything else, this practice shifts depending on my mood, the season of life I'm in, or what my spirit tells me I need. When I'm in need of deeper spiritual healing, I might pull a tarot or oracle card, read a daily prayer, and reflect on the reading for the day in my journal. I've found this practice to be so healing for me that I made a daily reader myself called *Look About You: A Book of Ordinary Prayers*. Writing it was its own beautiful spiritual test. I mean, how many ways can I say, "Hello, god, it's me Cody, and I want to connect with you." Apparently, I was able to do it 366 times, but what a test.

Above all else, spirituality is a way we can restore presence and tap into other realms and worlds so we may be more connected in this one. It demands that we look outside of our minds, beyond what the modern world would deem "logical," for guidance and answers. Though it can be challenging to trust at first, this Higher Power support provides relief from always trying to figure out what's next and solve problems on our own. We do not have to do this life alone; in fact, I argue that we weren't made to. We get to do it with other people and with the support of our spiritual practice.

As you work to gather the right tools for your spiritual toolbox in this chapter, you will also learn to cultivate stillness among the constant noise and distractions of the world. My hope is that, with these tools and insights, you will be able to read a stressful text message and center yourself through connection to your breath and spirit instead of getting worked up. Because here's the thing: You can remove every distraction possible, but interruptions and unforeseen circumstances will emerge whether you like it or not. You will have conflict, you will experience grief, you will have a new crush, change jobs, and make tough choices that inevitably pull you out of any Zen moment you were having. The good news is your spiritual practice always has the power to bring you back to yourself. And the more tools you can gather, the faster you can reorient yourself when people, places, and things attempt to throw you off course.

ACCEPTANCE AND SURRENDER

As I mentioned before, I've incorporated quite a few twelve-step concepts and principles into my life, and one of the big ones is the power of detaching with love and releasing my desire to control how my life goes. This takes a great deal of trust in my Higher Power to not take my own will back and always try to do things my way.

One spiritual tool that has really helped me with the concept of detachment is a "god box." A god box is any old box that you can fill with slips of paper. On these slips, you can write down whatever you are "turning over" or giving to god, whether it's fear, anxiety, or a negative thought. With this exercise, you're basically saying, "Here you go, god. I would like to stop worrying about this, and I will now let you control the outcome." Your slip of paper could say the name of a person, an idea you're struggling to let go of, or even a situation you've accepted is out of your hands. Maybe you are in the process of buying a house, so you write the address down and turn it over to god. The god box is a place to put all your fears, pains, and wishes so you can stop letting them distract you, and you can instead focus on what is in your control.

Other spiritual tools that have proven to be helpful for me are the concepts of acceptance and surrender. Surrendering is not the same as giving up, although it can feel very similar. Surrendering is the act of saying, "I have given this all I've got, and I now want to release my grip." It is saying, "I tried my best at controlling this outcome, and it's clearly above my pay grade so I am going to give it to god." Surrendering is complete freedom from control.

Acceptance, on the other hand, is trusting that, just for today, things are as they are for a reason. Things are as they should be. There is no way to change other people, places, or things, so by accepting them as they are, you will bring great peace into your life. You may also find you can love people more fully by accepting them as they are, and that changing them into a version of themselves that would make you feel safer actually doesn't provide the lessons that spirit has to offer you. Detachment, surrender, and acceptance—let these three words wash over you and become known to you in new ways. All three require action and trust in the universe, which has so much to give us and surprise us with.

PRAYER AS A SPIRITUAL PRACTICE FOR HEALING

Religious trauma is very real, and I acknowledge that the mention of prayer can bring up some unpleasant memories. For many people, especially queer and trans people, organized religion may have told you there was no place for you in it, but I want to reassure you that you are entitled to the benefits of prayer. A prayer practice can take many forms and can be as spontaneous or deliberate, as simple or complex, as you need it to be. I grew up in an agnostic home with parents who were not churchgoers and who encouraged me to believe in whatever I wanted, but I understand that this may not be the case for you. So a lot of this section may require you to reclaim certain things that you were told you didn't or shouldn't have access to.

Prayer, in its many forms, offers a deeply personal and transformative practice that helps us ground ourselves and reconnect with a higher purpose, so when we dip back into digital spaces, we are resourced and ready to take on whatever may come our way. Prayer offers an opportunity for us to vent, have a conversation with our Higher Power, or ask for protection for ourselves, people we love, people affected by crisis, and even people we resent if we choose. In fact, I've done a practice where I prayed twenty-one days for someone I resented to have a good day. I am not being dramatic when I say this was one of the hardest things I have ever done, but by the end, I was completely released of my obsessive resentment. Praying for other people in this way is a great way to think about yourself less and center those who need good energy.

Another prayer practice I did for over a year with friend, artist, and writer Sky Fusco was "the list," a practice we learned from Melody Beattie's book *Make Miracles in Forty Days*. For this exercise, she suggests you and a friend trade gratitude lists for forty days.

You include everything on the lists, not just the magical things you are grateful for, but the hard parts too. You might say, "I am grateful for my migraine because it forced me to cancel my day and actually take a break" or "I am grateful my partner didn't want to go to the movies with me because I had such a nice time alone." When we write out our gratitude as a reflection of the things that happened in the day, it transforms how we see the world and illuminates the beautiful surprises that may be in store for us. We loved it so much that we went beyond the forty days and did it daily for a year and a half.

Make your gratitude practice your own. Perhaps you'll feel more comfortable doing it alone or perhaps sharing it with others will inspire you to stay consistent. You could handwrite your list or text it to a friend. It can be done at any time of day to help you center yourself and refocus your attention on what matters most. Take a moment now to write down five things you're grateful for. Showing positive energy to the mundane things in your life signals to the universe that you're open for more. This too is a prayer.

Another practice you can add to your spiritual toolbox is an inventory practice where you take a factual look at your day. For this, I like to make two columns in my journal: Where did I let god in, and where did I not let god in? Or where did I take my will and control back and stop the flow, and where did I let the flow happen naturally? You can name your two columns something else, as long as you are observing what went well in the day and what needs adjusting tomorrow. Are there any amends that need to be made, big or small? Could you wake up a little earlier tomorrow to have time for your creative practice? Or do you need to sleep in and let yourself rest? This is the perfect place to honestly check in with yourself and god about how you can resolve and accept the day you had and look ahead to the next day, considering what might be worth shifting.

Prayer, in this way, is yet another moment of surrender, offering us a break from the constant demands of screens, responsibilities, and self-judgment. You could be in the middle of scrolling and close your eyes and just say, "God, please relieve me of the bondage of self. Please relieve me of the compulsion to keep scrolling. Please help me put my phone away and be of service to someone who could use a helping hand." Prayer is a way to cope with the digital and worldly burnout you are experiencing, offering a contemplative alternative that will get you centered.

Beyond daily prayers, gratitude lists, and inventories, you could also schedule time for ritual at the top of the week or month, every full moon, on pagan holidays, on the solstices, or whenever you want. Intention setting is its own form of prayer, making it clear to the universe what you want for yourself at this particular time. I find that when I get away from my spiritual practice, it is because I assume I am going to fail before I even try. But there's no way you can fail at something like this because it is all about your connection to your Higher Power. The practice is to call in what you want to see and experience, not make unreasonable demands of yourself or others.

MEDITATION AS A TOOL FOR RECLAIMING ATTENTION

I once famously wrote a newsletter titled "I DO NOT MEDITATE." It made a lot of people laugh, offended a few people, and made some people worry about me, but it is something I still stand by today somewhat, though I have shifted my tone around it a bit. Even though meditation is a newer part of my life, I have always deeply respected it as a part of religions, practices, and studies.

Meditation is a cornerstone of spiritual practice, offering a method to calm the mind, connect with the breath, heal from technology addiction, return to yourself, and restore your attention in the present moment. It is another gateway into the realm of peace with the self and peace with others, helping you become better equipped to face the tasks at hand both internally and externally. You may be coming into this with a preconceived notion of what meditation looks like. Perhaps a cross-legged pose, closed eyes, mudras, and a low "om" chant? Yes, this is one form of meditation, but your practice does not need to look exactly like this. Start small, in a position that feels most comfortable to you, and go from there. You can start with three minutes or even one minute. All that matters is that you don't overwhelm yourself and you build up to something that works for you.

If sitting meditation doesn't work for you, try a walking meditation or a guided meditation. There is no perfect way to meditate. Give yourself permission to find your own way and allow whatever wants to flow to you to come in. I have found that meditation can lead me to creative breakthroughs, clarity on a problem, or just offer my mind a chance to relax. This makes me a better writer, artist, and friend. I also find the biggest lesson is that it trains me to sit through discomfort and not reach for anything. A lot of what we have discussed so far is how to reach for something that isn't your phone, but what if we reached for nothing? What if we just sat still through the discomfort and the pain of not knowing? Or of knowing something deeply and not knowing if we are ready to face it? This is the gift of meditation. It expands our capacity to be uncomfortable and distracted without filling the god-sized hole with anything other than our acute attention to the breath.

SPIRITUALITY AND HEALING FROM TECHNOLOGY ADDICTION

Spirituality offers a pathway out of technology addiction, helping us cultivate healthier habits and relationships with the digital world. As you deepen your connection to your inner self and Higher Power, you will build more trust in your ability to put your phone down with more ease and less resistance. Our habits shift along with our trust in the universe, and the more we fill the god-sized hole with spiritual solutions, the less we keep grasping for straws hoping to find a little bit of connection in our tiny hand computers.

While technology can play a crucial role in our lives in countless ways, the disconnection and anxiety it causes can wreak havoc on our nervous systems.

But cultivating a spiritual practice has led me to less anxiety and more connection over time. I remember being so afraid that I wouldn't have any more friends when I left social media. I have not found this to be true. In fact, my friendships and relationships are more aligned than ever. Finding ways to pray, meditate, and cultivate contemplative practices give us the inner strength, fortitude, and belief in self to help us break free from the hold technology has over us. We can ask for divine intervention and guidance so we may be free of the ways that tech is designed to keep us hooked.

If you are still struggling to look away from your devices, try praying about it or meditating on the life you want to live instead. Try bringing it to your journal and turning it over to your Higher Power. There is no room for letting shame get in the way; bring the shame all the way into the process with you.

Getting in touch with your spiritual practice invites you to be more mindful and intentional about how you engage with technology—setting boundaries, practicing presence, and using digital tools as a means of connection rather than distraction. This process requires you to be kind to yourself and easy in the spirit. Do not try to push uphill; let it be an easy roll down. You also must be kind to yourself when you slip into old habits of overuse or distraction. This is part of the process. As technology and social media continue to grow and evolve, we will always have new things to resist. This is, after all, connected to whatever we are avoiding in the first place, so remember to bring your spiritual practice into that as well.

Healing from technology addiction is an ongoing endeavor, one that requires patience, consistency, and self-awareness, and giving yourself the gift of a spiritual practice offers the grounding support needed for lasting change. My hope is that you find methods that anchor you, remind you of your worth beyond the screen, and bring you back to what is real: the beautiful life you are building. May you feel your attention returning, slowly and steadily, to the people, places, and creative work that matters most. You do not have to do it perfectly; you just have to begin.

10

BEING OF SERVICE

Without community, there is no liberation.

—Audre Lorde, *The Master's Tools Will Never Dismantle the Master's House*

Everything in this book has led me to this chapter, the quiet center of my inquiry. This is what we should all shape our lives around: the gift of service. I have found that healing addiction, in any of its forms, is not necessarily through abstinence from the substance itself, but connection with others, and being of service is a wonderful way to build those connections and heal our attention, our communities, and our planet.

Being of service is at the threshold of creativity, research, spirituality, work, hobbies, and movement.

It lives at the intersection of the personal and the political and combines the private and public spheres. If we start to see our waking life as a continued series of opportunities to be of service, we will naturally want to be on our phones much less.

When you hear the word "service," you may think of participating in direct action or volunteering your time at a soup kitchen, shelter, or local farm, and while all of these are great examples, this is not the only way you can show up for your community. You can be of service to others by offering your artwork, knitting a hat for a friend, hosting a benefit art show, writing and performing a new song, or sharing any other piece of art with others. The root of service is giving people something to be inspired by and something that helps them see the world through a new lens. This is why we make art and indulge in our hobbies—for ourselves always, but also for the people.

When thinking of an entry point for service, I like to think of projects and practices that easily stem from the other things I feel passionate about. One writer who deeply inspires me is Rachel Cargle, who has started both a nonprofit organization and a bookstore. Out of her passion for wanting Black women and girls to be able to access therapy she started the Loveland Foundation, and out of her love for books, she started Elizabeth's Bookshop & Writing Centre in her hometown. Perhaps you want to start a small mobile bookshop in your town, or a project that is fiscally sponsored by Fractured Atlas while you look into nonprofit status. There are so many ways to take what lights you up and turn toward service.

SERVICE AS A HEALING PRACTICE

My favorite parts of having a digital-based business are all the ways I can be of service. For one, I make sure to provide offerings on a sliding scale so no one is turned away for lack of funds. For my writing group Landscapes, people pay on a sliding-scale model. Those who can pay more offset the cost of those who can pay less, and the average falls nicely somewhere in the middle. It makes for a lively and vibrant group, I get paid enough to feel good about the energy exchange, and together we're able to share resources with each other to support a more radical world.

My email newsletter is another central modality of my service practice. With it, I'm able to reach tens of thousands of people each week, and I take this responsibility really seriously. While I don't try to tackle every news event or world topic, I do often use it to share knowledge and links that could lead people to each other. Whether it is a GoFundMe after a wildfire, a local film screening about Palestine, one of my quilt raffles, a library book sale, resources to protect community members against ICE raids, or a Kickstarter for a friend's new music album, I use my platform to draw people's attention to what seems most pressing or healing in our current times.

Centering ourselves in service is of utmost importance in a world that often prioritizes individual success and digital connection over real, present relationships. Although a big portion of service is showing up for others, sometimes it means stepping aside and letting someone else lead. At the beginning of our dance classes, my mentors, The Architects, pose an intriguing question: Is it more generous to the dance to enter or to stay on the outside? Generosity isn't always about being in the mix; sometimes it's about framing the piece and letting others take the lead role. Everyone has their role in the web, and it's up to us to recognize what our role is in a particular moment and respect that.

I am not usually a person who likes crowds much. This used to make me feel bad for not attending protests, gatherings, or marches. But at some point, I accepted that my role is to be a writer—to write about the times we are living in and share resources using the platform and tools I do have. My role is also to support other activists and artists through one-on-one work where I often gift sessions or offer a sliding-scale rate, especially to those doing radical work on the ground. I can be a safe place to listen to others' concerns and validate what they're experiencing so they can go back out and do the integral work I don't feel comfortable doing. Whether you decide to be of service through community involvement, art-making, acts of friendship, or mutual aid, your role in the web is incredibly important and valid. And all of these acts work to heal our attention, as they demand a level of presence and heart that our phone screens do not.

Speaking of our screens, I want to briefly acknowledge how important social media has been for different political and social movements. We can talk a flip game about the art of the infographic, performative activism, and digital distractions, but social media has also been a vital gift, in that it is a free place for us to share information that is often hidden by mainstream media.

Choosing to continue to use social media to connect with friends, share information, and learn new things is nothing to be ashamed of. All I ask is that you be honest about how healthy your consumption is and adjust how you interact with it accordingly. It is my hope that service starts to fill your life so much that being on your phone for things outside of growth and development simply becomes less desirable. My hope is that you will continue to cultivate more focus in the moment and stay grounded in your real life so we can all be of service to each other without distractions.

Being of service within a community is not just about giving, but also receiving and creating mutual bonds that sustain long-term connections. You might grow old with the people you meet or you may need them in a crisis. Building these connections serves the people, but it also serves your well-being. We receive just as much as we give. This is the nourishing part of service: It can flow back to us.

Take some time now to write about what community means to you. What is the importance of real-life community in your day-to-day world? Maybe you'd just like to have someone you can sit on the couch and knit with. Your community and service work doesn't have to always be about saving and tending to the world. It is enough to desire community just to fill your cup so you can give back, survive, and sustain yourself. Community, at its core, is about being together in the rawness of life. Community as gathering, community as sinking into the couch, community as a foundation for service—all of this is grounded in love, trust, and authenticity.

BUILDING AND SUSTAINING COMMUNITIES OFFLINE IN A HYPER-ONLINE WORLD

In a hyper-connected digital world, building and sustaining real-world communities is an essential way to cultivate connection, healing, and meaningful service. To put it simply, staying off our screens allows us to be more tapped into what is happening right in our backyards. While major events that happen in other countries rightfully spark outrage in me and others, it often leads me to wonder what I could be directing my outrage to in my own community. What about protecting our Great Lakes from pipelines? What about the unhoused people in the encampment one town over? When I fight for causes that are happening around the world, how am I restoring justice in the place where I live instead of just bringing people's attention to what is happening everywhere else?

And on a separate note, do I need to even share what I am doing to be of service? Absolutely not. This work is not about proving something to an audience or even yourself. If anything, it is about removing yourself from the situation so you may be available as an additional resource. Everything in this book up until now has been about resourcing the self, and we do this so we can be of service to others in return. That's the natural human flow. Resource the self, then resource others.

Like we discussed in chapter 3, technology often creates the illusion of connection while also contributing to isolation and disconnection. While I find so much value in texting and video-calling my friends, living in a small rural town as a nonbinary queer person made me realize just how small my community was. Not only did I realize how much I needed to communicate with my chosen kin who lived elsewhere, but also that I needed to engage with podcasts, audiobooks, and news shows.

Finding that balance between connecting through the phone and being without social media and email was a godsend that truly changed my life and attention span. I know it can seem overwhelming to not have unfettered access to social media, but nothing is more satisfying than connecting offline with friends and family.

As you begin implementing the practices you've learned throughout this book, you'll find that you naturally gravitate to your phone less. Continue to keep an eye on your attention as you build in these new tools and see where it goes. You may be surprised at how opportunities to build community and be of service present themselves to you.

WAYS TO BUILD COMMUNITY OFFLINE

Building community in person doesn't have to be difficult or stressful, and you don't necessarily need to be
in contact with tons of people. Your circle of friends,
your book club, or the regulars you chat with at your
local coffee shop are all examples of community. Any
relationships you can foster with others is enough to
reap the positive benefits of service.

HOSTING OR ATTENDING GATHERINGS

Hosting or attending events—whether small dinners,
community events, or group meetups—nourishes
attention, fosters presence, and deepens connection.
Try having a potluck at your house or organize an art
auction at the community center. Even if you don't
consider yourself a leader or a self-starter in this way,
you can propose something small and see it grow from
there. Perhaps you want to host a writer's group at your
house where everyone reads something they've been
working on. Maybe you can attend a quilt guild to meet
and hang out with people from the next generation and
introduce them to the idea of raffling off their quilts for
a little radical action.

Using the home as a gathering space can be so vital
to community because it's a resource you already
have in your back pocket. You could host a rotating
dinner club with friends, turn your yard into an out-
door movie theatre with a sheet and a cheap projector,
host traveling poets for a zine reading, invite people
over for a natural dye workshop—anything you're

interested in. You can, of course, use digital portals to tell people about your events, but also consider making flyers and putting them up at food co-ops, coffee shops, cafes, campgrounds, or trail heads. And if you are not one to organize alone, ask a friend to do it with you. Or, if you aren't ready or interested in starting your own thing, pay attention to the fliers posted on local bulletin boards to see if there's a group you want to join or an event you'd like to attend. I also have found a lot of luck in local Discord groups, especially for trans and nonbinary people.

FRIENDSHIP: THE HEART OF SERVICE

A big question writers often face is, "How much do I consider the audience before I write, and how much do I just consider myself?" My answer to this lands somewhere in the middle. When I write my newsletter, I often ask myself, "What do my friends need this week?" I think of those I have spoken to recently, what they've been interested in, and what they're reading, working on, and paying attention to. I think about any challenges they may have faced that week and what resources or storytelling could be helpful to them. Of course I am writing what is of interest to me, but I am also writing for the people. When I tune into one to three friends as I write my newsletter, it gives me a prototype audience to speak to through my writing.

Using this method inadvertently requires me to nurture my friendships throughout the week, not as a way to mine material for my newsletter, but as a way to pay attention to the world outside of digital spaces.

True friendship thrives on presence, shared attention, and vulnerability, and being of service to our friends is one of the most meaningful ways we can connect with them. A huge way I connect with my closest friends is through the mail. We mail each other the books we write, gifts around big anniversaries or launches, letters, postcards, art, and more. It is one of my favorite ways to connect with my friends that has seemingly lost favor in our digital world.

Another entry point to connection I love is picking up the phone to call a friend to ask them how *they* are doing when I am spiraling about something in my own life. I turn the focus away from myself, not because I don't care about myself, but because I often fall too far down the trap of wanting to "fix" everything about my life instead of just living inside of it. Asking someone else how they are doing usually snaps me out of my self-obsession and into service mode, giving me an opportunity to practice being a good listener and a good friend. More often than not, the friend will eventually ask how I am doing, and I will have an opportunity to share what's been coming up for me. Usually by the time I have listened to my friend, my nervous system has calmed down and my spiral is less intense. Presence is truly the most valuable gift.

MUTUAL AID: COLLECTIVE CARE AND RESOURCE SHARING

Mutual aid is a powerful form of service that centers on collective care, resource sharing, and the understanding that we are all interconnected and responsible for each other's well-being. When the COVID-19 pandemic began, we saw a rise in mutual aid efforts in a new and unprecedented way. This paired with a spotlight on the Black Lives Matter movement after the murders of George Floyd and Breonna Taylor, among dozens of other Black people killed by police every year.

In so many ways, we have technology to thank for this. I held multiple raffles and fundraisers on social media, raising thousands of dollars to redistribute to different organizations, and GoFundMes and Kickstarters continue to change people's lives. While we can use email newsletters and our local community to share and disperse information, this is where social media can really shine as a tool and a resource. The trick is to just use it for its functionality—to make a post, share a raffle, or donate to someone's cause—and not get hooked in by the dopamine loop it can spin us into.

Of course, mutual aid has existed way before 2020 and even the advent of the internet. One of the ways collective funds were raised in the past was through art raffles and auctions. When looking for ways to get involved in your community, start with your creative practice. Quilts were my personal entry point, and they, along with other textile art, have been used as tools of activism for decades, if not centuries. The book *Radical Tradition*, a catalogue of quilts from the Toledo Museum of Art, gives beautiful examples of quilts that were used in fundraisers dating back to the Civil and Vietnam wars. Don't ever think your creative work is not enough to move the needle; I assure you, it is more than enough. Find your entry point, keep an eye out for calls for art, or donate your time to causes that speak to you. I've given away many one-on-one sessions or classes as a part of fundraising efforts.

Mutual aid can also be woven into the fabric of our everyday lives. It might look like cooking for a friend who just had top surgery or a baby, checking in with neighbors during a snowstorm or power outage, offering a ride to someone who doesn't have a vehicle, or dropping off unused items to a local shelter or thrift store. These acts might seem small or insignificant, but they add up and are a living practice of community care. They remind us that tending to one another outside of transactional systems is not just meaningful, but necessary for our collective survival.

Everyday mutual aid is a revolutionary response to systems that have failed us. In moments of crisis, from pandemics to climate collapse, it is our interdependence that ensures survival. You do not have to do everything alone; in fact, this individualistic mindset is counterintuitive and will only slow you down. Practicing mutual aid disrupts this myth of individualism. It shifts our mindset out of competition to one of care, where resources, time, and attention are shared. It is a way of building the world we long for, one act of solidarity at a time.

REFLECT

- What acts of care have others extended to you that felt deeply meaningful or restorative?

- What skills, resources, or time do you have that could be shared in small and/or consistent ways?

- Who in your community might benefit from your actions?

- What would it look like to integrate mutual aid into your creative practice?

- How does it feel to imagine care as a form of resistance?

Let this be a space to dream of what is possible and notice what you already practice and can easily fold into your life.

THE IMPACT OF SERVICE ON OUR ATTENTION AND PRESENCE

Service to others restores our attention by pulling us out of the digital haze and placing our focus on the real-world needs of the people around us. It is a fast-acting way to become more committed to the self, other people, and the needs of the Earth. As we've discussed, there are many ways you can be of service, whether you become a member of a community garden, donate to a local Indigenous organization, or volunteer with a local group. With so many options available and so many groups needing assistance, it can be difficult to know where to start and where your skills and resources are of most benefit.

To decide how and where to contribute to your community, take a moment in your journal to ask yourself:

- What are my desires?
- What am I interested in?
- What would keep me interested long enough to stay consistent?
- Which of my skills could benefit an organization?

For instance, maybe you are great at writing grants or copywriting and you want to help a local organization start a monthly newsletter. Or maybe you're great at drawing and thinking of impactful chants so you partner with a local group to help design their protest signs. Think of all the skills you have built with your hobbies and work and how they could be of benefit to others.

It's important to note that you don't always have to be of service for free. I am firmly rooted in knowing that my full-price business offerings are also a form of service. It is a way for me to let my gifts be of service to others while being compensated for my time and energy. Whether you're good at caring for animals, writing, dancing, or teaching, your skills can be used for good and deserve to be compensated. It doesn't always have to be one or the other. You don't have to turn every part of your business into a sliding-scale pricing model, but it's nice to have at least one offering that is more accessible but still contributes to your livelihood. This is not only an act of service, but it also brings more people into your ecosystem for connection, care, and reciprocity.

Service also helps you battle the need for constant productivity. You are already doing enough, so sometimes your service work will be rooted in seeing where there are opportunities to add in more generosity or notice where you are already being generous. If anything, you might need to turn down some of your generosity if you are overextending yourself during times when you need to be less available to the people.

I find that my availability of service occurs in waves, depending on how much work I have going on, how demanding my schoolwork is on any given week, and what my physical and mental capacity is. Make sure you don't burn yourself out in the process of weaving service into your life. The point is not to add more for you to do, but to instead add value and connection into your life. And sometimes, you may find that you actually need to add something in that allows for more generosity, healing, and reconnection. Regardless, acts of service are a way to foster a sense of devotion and purpose in your life and work.

Finally, service offers us a way to be grateful—for our life, our friendships, and our community connections.

It offers a way for us to deepen our other practices, including a spiritual practice. You might not be religious, but I always encourage people to look up events at their local Unitarian Universalist church. These spaces are often doing radical organizing work, hosting cool events and talks, and are committed to giving back to the community. Twelve-step organizations like Alcoholics Anonymous, Al-Anon, and Debtors Anonymous are other free spaces where you can find like-minded community members to process emotions and life with. You could even reach out to organizations like Gilda's Club, for people and family members affected by cancer; grief groups at the library; or other spaces that focus on emotional support and healing.

Whether you are starting something new or finding your way toward something that already exists, your attention to self and the world around you will continue to sharpen through acts of service. You will find yourself in more alignment with your purpose and your community, which can bring you closer to your Higher Power. Becoming one with your creator, no matter what that looks like to you, comes about when you integrate all your tools in a selfless way.

SERVICE AND MONEY WORK AS TOOLS FOR EMOTIONAL REGULATION

Once I had all of these systems in place—hobbies, movement, creativity, research, spirituality, and service— my life, including my seemingly never-ending debt, became so much more manageable. Today, I keep track of my numbers in a budgeting app, and specifically I have found YNAB to be what works best for me. I enter them manually every day, so I have the experience of touching in with every purchase I make and identifying if it worked for me or not. And I have a spreadsheet with a spending plan for both my personal expenses and my business so I can visually see the patterns that have emerged, as well as a page for my projected income.

I also have experimented with spending bans, which helped me to finally start saving, chip away at my six figures—yes . . . six figures—of tax debt, and pay myself a salary at the top of each month. Today as I type this, I am financially solvent for the first time in twelve years of self-employment, and I can absolutely say that by being solvent, I am able to be more of service. I am less stressed, more available to the people I love, and able to offer greater presence to those I care about most.

Now, you may be wondering what personal finances has to do with service, and to that I say, good question. For a long time, my relationship with my finances caused me so much stress. I was disorganized with my bookkeeping, chronically underearning, and compulsively overspending to the point where all my spare energy went into either dealing with or avoiding my financial situation. The shame that came along with this kept me in a constant state of disconnection and distraction, and it wasn't until I got a handle on it, thanks to my friend Nic Antoinette and one of their amazing classes on money, that I was able to see just how much of an impact this had on every aspect of my life, most notably my connection to service and community.

Over the course of several months, I had to get very honest with myself about why I continued to foster my negative relationship with money, how it was affecting my life, and what I was willing to do to step out of this pattern and finally do something different. It wasn't easy, and it required a lot of tough self-reflection and lifestyle changes, like restructuring the way I ran my business, getting organized with spreadsheets, and committing to using a budget tracker.

These shifts weren't just about numbers; they were about reclaiming clarity and stability in my internal world. When my finances are in chaos, my mind is too. I was constantly distracted, anxious, and unable to be fully present with myself or others. I couldn't truly show up in service because I was always operating from a place of scarcity—even if I did have enough—because I wasn't taking a clear stock of what I had.

As I built more structure into my financial life, I noticed I had more capacity—more energy to give and create and more groundedness to support others in my work and personal life. Healing my relationship with money will continue to be a lifelong pursuit, but it has become a way for me to be of greater service to my community, and it helps me move through the world with more intention and integrity. I continue this work today with the help of my therapist and many guides, including Hadassah Damien of Ride Free Fearless Money who has truly transformed my mindset and skillset around money.

While the budgeting apps and spreadsheets worked wonders in getting me to a better financial position, what really helped me regulate my emotions around money was implementing a spending plan and ban. It's interesting. My out-of-control spending and emotional dysregulation got way worse when I quit social media. Quitting social media the way I did often reminds me of when I quit drinking or quit smoking cigarettes—not just the withdrawal symptoms, but the reality that using these substances actually helped me take a load off. Even though they were unhealthy habits for me, they had a purpose in temporarily filling that god-sized hole. So when I stopped using social media, I noticed I was still chasing that same dopamine hit through my spending habits.

The first time I ever did a spending ban was for six weeks in the fall of 2024. My biggest rules were no books, no plants, no clothes, and no home decor. But that doesn't mean I didn't find ways to acquire those things through trading and the gift economy. This wasn't my intention at all, but my spending ban brought me closer to my desires and the people in my life. I know budgeting, spending plans, and spending bans can start to mimic diet culture, so please be mindful when you approach anything with too much black-and-white thinking. These tools are meant to bring more presence and healed attention, not less.

At the end of the day, emotional regulation is what we are aiming for in all parts of our lives. It's what can bring us into alignment with our attention because it's ultimately what we are aiming for when we choose to numb out on our phones. When you get a handle on your emotions and put a stop to your reckless spending, you'll find that you have a greater capacity to actively engage in other aspects of your life, service included. Sometimes service is the antidote to self-absorption. By stepping outside our own challenges and focusing on the needs of others, we gain clarity and release our own negative emotions. In this way, service acts as a form of emotional regulation that reconnects us to both our emotional health and our capacity for giving.

BUILDING A LIFELONG PRACTICE OF SERVICE

As we wind down here, I encourage you to think of your practice of service as a lifelong offering, meaning it's important that you don't burn out. Make space in your schedule so you can have entire days to yourself with absolutely no commitments; full days where you aren't on your computer; days of less stress, more creativity, more attention, and less fractured focus; and days of heartfelt connection and soul-nourishing service.

Whether it is through small acts of kindness, a text to a friend, your art, mutual aid, or volunteer work, I encourage you to make service a consistent and easeful part of your life. It is a practice of presence that fills our time so we do not have to be so hooked on distractions that keep us disconnected. See your personal work, both private and public, as an entry point to connection, and integrate every piece of this work we've done together into your life. You might just be at the starting point, but the more you practice the principles of this book in all your efforts, the more you will be met with great rewards—the rewards of community, friendship, creativity, joy, and a life truly worth living. May service begin at home, with rest as its first offering. May service keep us in right relationship with money, time, and body. May service be maintenance as much as miracle.

CONCLUSION

Throughout this book, we've asked ourselves what we are avoiding. We've examined the many small fractures in our attention and explored how digital noise, endless demands, and systemic pressures fragment us. Together, we've practiced reclaiming our attention, piece by piece, through movement, creativity, service, and the gentle discipline of noticing where we are and what we want to tend to. These practices are not one-time fixes or boxes to check off. They are ongoing relationships. The practice of attention is not about getting it perfect; it's about returning, again and again, to what matters most.

At this point, you may be wondering, *What now?* Now, you keep practicing. You keep turning the dial up by 1 percent, noticing where you want to pivot, and allowing yourself to live the experiment of a more attentive life. So, how do you do this? How do you begin to embody the practices we've uncovered together?

This is where the idea of integration comes in. Whether it be day by day, an artist residency, a fleeting afternoon, or a self-led solo retreat—it should be viewed not as a grand escape, but as a quiet return. This integration period, whether it's a few early mornings at your kitchen table or a weekend away in a modest motel, can give your attention room to breathe. It can help you step outside the swirl of routine and see your patterns and desires with fresh eyes.

When I finished this book, I crafted an at-home retreat, waking early each morning to write before the world asked anything of me. I let myself relax when needed, adjusted my rules, and moved between writing, hobbies, and walking outside. It wasn't about perfection; it was about creating a container for clarity to arrive.

If you need new scenery to spark your creativity, you can host a solo retreat outside the home as well. A cute, cheap motel up the street will do. Taking yourself outside of your normal routine and atmosphere even for two nights can help all your ideas come together. You can mind map all over the walls of your house or rental and dream up how your practices can come together. Buy a giant sticky note pad and put paper all over the walls. Write out your income streams, your marketing ideas. List your practices: hobbies, creativity, movement, spirituality, and service. How will you integrate them? How will it all come together? You can start with your attention audit, then determine the best path forward for a digital detox.

PLANNING A SOLO RETREAT

Here are some tips to get you started in planning a solo retreat or integration period:

- Decide on the length of time. A minimum of three days will give you plenty of time and space.
- You don't have to take off work! I worked and taught regular hours during my at-home writing retreat.
- Plan time for your creative practice/art-making; the earlier the better. The biggest benefit to waking up early is you can dive into your practice before people start to enter your inbox or gather on Zoom.
- Make a decision about media. What will you consume, what will you leave behind, what will you take in?

Regardless of whether or not you choose to do a formal retreat, the real work of attention happens in your daily life. Every moment you choose presence over distraction, every time you close a tab and take a breath, every time you make a decision that honors your values, you're engaging in this practice.

Attention, as we've explored together, is not only about what we focus on, but also how we relate to the world. It's how we choose to meet each moment—with resistance or with curiosity, with avoidance or with a willingness to see what's there. It's how we notice the small thresholds in our day: the moment before we pick up our phone, our breath before we speak, the quiet pull toward rest that we often override.

In a culture that rewards constant output and distraction, choosing to live attentively is a radical act. It is a way of saying, "I will not abandon myself in the rush to be productive, visible, or acceptable. I will not abandon what is alive in me for what seems urgent but is actually unimportant." It is a way of saying yes to your life as it is while still making space for the changes you long for.

You will inevitably lose your attention again along the way. You will scroll when you want to write, numb out when you want to move, overcommit when you mean to rest. That's okay. Attention is a practice because it requires returning, not because it requires perfection. When you notice yourself drifting, you can begin again. You can close the laptop, step outside, take a breath, and remember that you are allowed to begin again as many times in a day as you need.

You can also let this practice ripple outward. The more you reclaim your attention, the more you can be present for your relationships, creative work, and commitments to the world. Your presence can become a quiet offering, a stabilizing force for yourself and others. When we practice attention, we practice care. We practice connection. We practice becoming the kind of people who can meet the world, and each other, with clarity and kindness.

So, as you close this book and reenter life, keep practicing, keep returning, and trust that even the smallest moments of attention matter. They all add up to shape your days, which inevitably shape your life.

Thank you for allowing me to walk beside you in this practice. May you find spaciousness, clarity, and courage as you continue to reclaim your attention, and may your attention guide you back to the life you want to live—again and again.

RESOURCES

I began work on this book in 2021 shortly after I saw the documentary *The Social Dilemma*. In many ways it confirmed what I already knew about my relationship to my phone, and specifically to social media apps.

While this book doesn't have formal footnotes or a bibliography it felt important to name every book I read, combed through, stumbled upon, quoted, or came to for guidance. It is my hope that these books bring you even deeper into the work.

BOOKS

Etel Adnan, *Sea and Fog*

Nic Antoinette, *How to Be Alone*

Nic Antoinette, *What We Owe to Ourselves*

Lauren Applebaum, *Radical Tradition: American Quilts and Social Change*

Adam Atler, *Irresistible: The Rise of Addictive Technology and the Business of Keeping Us Hooked*

Melody Beattie, *Make Miracles in Forty Days*

Melody Beattie, *The Language of Letting Go*

Billy-Ray Belcourt, *A History of My Brief Body*

Mia Birdsong, *How We Show Up: Reclaiming Family, Friendship, and Community*

Grace Lee Boggs and Scott Kurashige, *The Next American Revolution: Sustainable Activism for the Twenty-First Century*

Oliver Burkeman, *Four Thousand Weeks: Time Management for Mortals*

Julia Cameron, *The Artist's Way*

Julia Cameron, *Walking in This World: The Practical Art of Creativity*

Rachel E. Cargle, *A Renaissance of Our Own: A Memoir & Manifesto on Reimagining*

Pema Chödrön, *When Things Fall Apart*

Ram Dass, *Be Here Now*

Ram Dass, *Journey of Awakening: A Meditator's Guidebook*

Paco de Leon, *Finance for the People: Getting a Grip on Your Finances*

Diane di Prima, *Revolutionary Letters*

Jessica Dore, *Tarot for Change*

Melissa Febos, *Body Work*

Tiago Forte, *The PARA Method: Simplify, Organize, and Master Your Digital Life*

Susan Leigh Foster, *Dances That Describe Themselves: The Improvised Choreography of Richard Bull*

Ross Gay, *The Book of Delights*

Jean Genet, *Our Lady of the Flowers*

Elizabeth Gilbert, *Big Magic*

Allen Ginsberg, *Howl and Other Poems*

Jocelyn K. Glei, *Unsubscribe: How to Kill Email Anxiety, Avoid Distractions, and Get Real Work Done*

Natalie Goldberg, *Writing Down the Bones*

Isabella Hammad, *Recognizing the Stranger: On Palestine and Narrative*

Thich Nhat Hanh, *The Miracle of Mindfulness: An Introduction to the Practice of Meditation*

Johann Hari, *Stolen Focus*

Kelly Hayes and Mariame Kaba, *Let This Radicalize You*

bell hooks, *Teaching to Transgress*

Fenton Johnson, *At the Center of All Beauty*

Briona Simone Jones (Ed.), *Mouths of Rain: An Anthology of Black Lesbian Thought*

Cleve Jones, *When We Rise: My Life in the Movement*

Erling Kagge, *Walking: One Step at a Time*

Jack Kerouac and Allen Ginsberg, (Bill Morgan and David Stanford, Eds.), *The Letters*

Rashid Khalidi, *The Hundred Years' War on Palestine*

Robin Wall Kimmerer, *Braiding Sweetgrass*

Robin Wall Kimmerer, *The Serviceberry*

Liz Koch, *Stalking Wild Psoas: Embodying Your Core Intelligence*

Petra Kuppers, *Eco Soma*

Joanne Kyger, *Strange Big Moon: The Japan and India Journals, 1960–1964*

Joanne Kyger (Cedar Sigo, Ed.), *There You Are: Interviews, Journals, and Ephemera*

Anna Lembke, *Dopamine Nation: Finding Balance in the Age of Indulgence*

Kate Levinson, *Emotional Currency*

Audre Lorde, *Sister Outsider*

Stephanie Loveless (Ed.), *A Year of Deep Listening: 365 Text Scores for Pauline Oliveros*

Katherine May, *Wintering*

Bernadette Mayer, *Memory*

Cait McKinney, *Information Activism:
A Queer History of Lesbian Media
Technologies (Sign, Storage, Transmission)*

Resmaa Menakem, *My Grandmother's Hands*

Larry Mitchell and Ned Asta (Illus.), *The
Faggots & Their Friends Between
Revolutions*

Cal Newport, *Deep Work*

Safiya Umoja Noble, *Algorithms of Oppression*

Mary Oliver, *Devotions*

Sally Palaian, *Spent: Break the Buying
Obsession and Discover Your True Worth*

Wendy Perron, *The Grand Union: Accidental
Anarchists of Downtown Dance*

Ethan Philibrick, *Group Works: Art, Politics,
and Collective Ambivalence*

Carl Phillips, *My Trade is Mystery*

Leah Lakshmi Piepzna-Smarashinha, *Care Work: Dreaming Disability Justice*

Joseph Pilates, *Return to Life Through Contrology*

Rachel Pollack, *Seventy-Eight Degrees of Wisdom*

Carrot Quinn, *Thru-Hiking Will Break Your Heart*

Yvonne Rainer, *Feelings Are Facts: A Life*

Fariha Róisín, *Who is Wellness For?*

Mark Rosenthal, *Diego Rivera & Frida Kahlo in Detroit*

Legacy Russell, *Glitch Feminism: A Manifesto*

Richard C. Schwartz, *No Bad Parts*

Assata Shakur, *Assata: An Autobiography*

Erin Sharkey, *A Darker Wilderness: Black Nature Writing from Soil to Stars*

Raja Shehadeh, *Palestinian Walks*

Naomi Shimada and Sarah Raphael, *Mixed
Feelings: The Emotional Impact of Our
Digital Habits*

Rebecca Solnit, *Wanderlust*

Dean Spade, *Mutual Aid*

Bari Tessler, *The Art of Money*

Twyla Tharp, *The Creative Habit*

Heather Ann Thompson, *Blood in the Water:
The Attica Prison Uprising of 1971 and Its
Legacy*

Anne Waldman and Emma Gomis (Eds.), *New
Weathers: Poetics from the Naropa Archive*

Meggan Watterson, *Mary Magdalene
Revealed*

Simone Weil, *Gravity and Grace*

Simone Weil, *Waiting for God*

Shawn Wilson, *Research Is Ceremony:
Indigenous Research Methods*

Shoshana Zuboff, *The Age of Surveillance
Capitalism*

APPS

Brick

JOMO

SelfControl

Wisephone

PODCASTS AND LISTENING

Democracy Now!

Mother Country Radicals

Off the Grid with Amelia Hruby

KEEPING IN TOUCH

Thank you for reading *The Practice of Attention*.
There are many ways that you can keep in touch, spread the word about this book, and join my creative ecosystem.

Visit: Go to thepracticeofattention.com for links to buy the book, free resources, press, and the most up-to-date news on events, workshops, and more.

Stay in the loop: Find my digital world at codycookparrott.com including options to

Subscribe to my weekly newsletter; landing in your inbox since 2012, I write personal essays on attention, devotion, queerness, creative practice, values-based business, rural living, and my wildest thoughts on love

Listen to my podcast, *Common Shapes*

Join one of my co-working groups

Book a creative advising session

Take my classes on creative practice

Download free resources

Peruse the archive

And more

Be in touch:

Send me an email at
info@codycookparrott.com

Mail me a letter at
PO Box 252, Cedar, MI 49621

Tell people this book exists:

Leave an online review: Leaving online reviews is like a small love letter and I would love to see what you think of the book.

Invite me to be on your podcast or interview me in your newsletter: I'd love to talk about leaving social media, starting an email newsletter from scratch, being nonbinary in a small town, and anything we can think of together.

Share a photo of the book on a social media channel you aren't addicted to.

Write about it in your newsletter and forward me the email—I'd love to read it.

Text a friend the link to buy their own copy.

Ask your local bookstore or library to order it.

Invite me to give a talk at your speaking event—I am very funny and have prepared a whole talk about the book. I would love to speak to your coworkers about attention, social media addiction, and tuning in to their writing practice.

Invite me to your book club.

ACKNOWLEDGMENTS

My gratitude is endless. Thank you to:

My agents, Rebecca Gradinger and Madison Hernick, for shaping the frame and pushing me to my edges.

My editors, Sarah Stanton, Lyric Dodson, Jade Lascelles, and Sara Veglahn. You took my wild sentences and big ideas and made them make sense. Thank you for making this book a book.

The entire team at Sounds True.

Nova Evermore, for early reading and feedback.

Merray Michael Mina, for encouraging me to celebrate finishing a first draft.

Kate Henry, for the gift of the pomodoro method and gentle productivity.

Landscapes, the greatest writing group I could ask for.

Tamara Santibañez, my true hype guy when I questioned my role in the great ecosystem.

All of my friends—without you I am nothing.

My family, thank you for never questioning me as an artist.

My love, Kathryn Rhiannon Campbell, thank you for your endless support.

Nic Antoinette and Amelia Hruby, for showing me that a world without Instagram was possible.

And the many fellows, friends, readers, students, and companions who lift my spirit every day, thank you from the bottom of my heart. Your support means the world to me.

ABOUT THE AUTHOR

Cody Cook-Parrott is an artist, writer, and movement practitioner living on the Leelanau Peninsula in Northern Michigan. They write a weekly newsletter and host the podcast *Common Shapes*. They build simple structures that help artists make work. Their focus is attention, creative ecosystems, and research—so the practice becomes a scaffolding to grow steadily—online and off.

Cody holds a BFA in Dance from the University of Michigan and works with improvisation as a compositional method through all modalities—specifically movement, quilting, and writing. Their dance project, Personal Practice, has been featured in the *New York Times*, *Dance Magazine*, *Vanity Fair*, and more.

ABOUT SOUNDS TRUE BOOKS

Sounds True was founded in 1985 by Tami Simon with a clear mandate: to disseminate spiritual wisdom. Since starting out as a project with one woman and her tape recorder, Sounds True has grown into a mission-driven learning and media company, partnering with many of the leading wisdom teachers and visionaries of our time.

Every Sounds True Book is designed to not only provide information to a reader but to also to embody the quality of a wisdom transmission, unlocking our greatest capacities to love, serve, and uplift others.

Sounds True Books are part of St. Martin's Essentials, an imprint of Macmillan Publishers.

**ST. MARTIN'S
ESSENTIALS
NEW YORK**